Insects

of the North Woods

T0151125

Insects
of the North Woods

By Jeffrey Hahn

Kollath+Stensaas
P u b l i s h i n g

Kollath+Stensaas Publishing
394 Lake Avenue South, Suite 406
Duluth, MN 55802
Office: 218.727.1731
Orders: 800.678.7006
info@kollathstensaas.com
www.kollathstensaas.com

INSECTS *of the* NORTH WOODS

Printed in South Korea by Doosan
10 9 8 7 6 5 4 3 2

Editorial Director: Mark Sparky Stensaas
Graphic Designer: Rick Kollath

ISBN-13: 978-0-9792006-4-9

Table of Contents

What is an Insect?	**1**
How to Enjoy Insects	**5**
How to Use this Field Guide	**18**

Springtails (Collembola) — **10–11**

Mayflies (Ephemeroptera) — **12–13**

Dragonflies & Damselflies (Odonata) — **14–22**

Darners (*Aeshnidae*)	16	Skimmers (*Libellulidae*)	19
Clubtails (*Gomphidae*)	17	Damselflies (*Zygoptera*)	22
Emeralds (*Cordulidae*)	18		

Stoneflies (Plecoptera) — **23–25**

Grasshoppers, Katydids & Crickets (Orthoptera) — **26–37**

Grasshoppers (*Acrididae*)	28	Crickets (*Gryllidae*)	36
Pygmy Grasshoppers (*Tetrigidae*)	33	Camel Crickets (*Rhaphidophoridae*)	37
Katydids (*Tettigonidae*)	34		

Walkingsticks (Phasmida) — **38–39**

Earwigs (Dermaptera) — **40–41**

Cockroaches (Blattaria) — **42–43**

True Bugs, Cicadas, Hoppers, etc (Hemiptera) — **44–77**

Water Scorpions (*Nepidae*)	46	Leaf-footed Bugs (*Coreidae*)	61
Giant Water Bugs (*Belostomatidae*)	47	Broad-headed Bugs (*Alydidae*)	62
Water Boatmen (*Corixidae*)	48	Scentless Plant Bugs (*Rhopalidae*)	63
Backswimmers (*Notonectidae*)	49	Stink Bugs (*Pentatomidae*)	64
Water Striders (*Gerridae*)	50	Parent Bugs (*Acanthosomatidae*)	66
Shore Bugs (*Saldidae*)	51	Shield Bugs (*Scutelleridae*)	67
Lace Bugs (*Tingidae*)	52	Cicadas (*Cicadidae*)	68
Plant Bugs (*Miridae*)	53	Acanaloniid Planthoppers (*Acanaloniidae*)	69
Damsel Bugs (*Nabidae*)	56	Flatid Planthoppers (*Flatidae*)	69
Minute Pirate Bugs (*Anthocoridae*)	57	Treehoppers (*Membracidae*)	70
Ambush/Assassin Bugs (*Reduviidae*)	58	Froghoppers (Spittlebugs) (*Cercopidae*)	72
Stilt Bugs (*Berytidae*)	60	Leafhoppers (*Cicidellidae*)	74
Seed Bugs (*Lygaeidae*)	60	Aphids (*Aphididae*)	76

Booklice & Bark lice (Psocoptera) — **78–79**

Beetles (Coleoptera)   80–131

Ground & Tiger Beetles (*Carabidae*)	82	Dermestid Beetles (*Dermestidae*)	105
Whirligig Beetles (*Gyrinidae*)	88	Soldier Beetles (*Cantharidae*)	106
Predaceous Diving Beetles (*Dytiscidae*)	89	Checkered Beetles (*Cleridae*)	107
Water Scavenger Beetles (*Hydrophilidae*)	90	Ladybird Beetles (*Coccinellidae*)	108
Clown Beetles (*Histeridae*)	91	Sapfeeding Beetles (*Nitidulidae*)	111
Carrion Beetles (*Silphidae*)	92	Wedge-shaped Beetles (*Ripiphoridae*)	112
Rove Beetles (*Staphylinidae*)	94	Flat Bark Beetles (*Cucujidae*)	112
Stag Beetles (*Lucanidae*)	95	Tumbling Flower Beetles (*Mordellidae*)	113
Earth-boring Dung Beetles (*Geotrupidae*)	96	Darkling Beetles (*Tenebrionidae*)	114
Scarab Beetles (*Scarabaeidae*)	97	Fire-colored Beetles (*Pyrochroidae*)	115
Metallic Wood-boring Beetles (*Buprestidae*)	100	Blister Beetles (*Meloidae*)	116
Click Beetles (*Elateridae*)	102	Leaf Beetles (*Chrysomelidae*)	118
Net-winged Beetles (*Lycidae*)	103	Long-horned Beetles (*Cerambycidae*)	124
Fireflies (*Lampyridae*)	104	Weevils (*Curculionidae*)	129

Alderflies, Dobsonflies & Lacewings (Neuroptera)   132–139

Alderflies (*Sialidae*)	134	Brown Lacewings (*Hemerobiidae*)	137
Dobsonflies & Fishflies (*Corydalidae*)	135	Green Lacewings (*Chrysopidae*)	138
Mantidflies (*Mantispidae*)	136	Antlions (*Myrmeleontidae*)	139

Sawflies, Wasps, Bees & Ants (Hymenoptera)   140–165

Cimbicid Sawflies (*Cimbicidae*)	142	Digger Wasps (*Crabroninae*)	154
Horntails (*Siricidae*)	143	Thread-waisted Wasps (*Sphecidae*)	156
Common Sawflies (*Tenthredinidae*)	144	Cuckoo Wasps (*Chrysididae*)	159
Ichneumon Wasps (*Ichneumonidae*)	146	Velvet Ants (*Mutillidae*)	159
Pelecinid Wasps (*Pelecinidae*)	149	Ants (*Formicidae*)	160
Leaf-cutter Bees (*Megachilidae*)	150	Spider Wasps (*Pompilidae*)	162
Halictid Bees (Sweat Bees) (*Halictidae*)	151	Gasteruptiid Wasps (*Gasteruptiidae*)	163
Honey Bees, Bumble Bees (*Apidae*)	152	Yellowjackets, Hornets (*Vespidae*)	164

Caddisflies (Trichoptera)   166–169

Butterflies & Moths (Lepidoptera)   170–191

Swallowtails (*Papilionidae*)	172	Hooktip Moths (*Drepanidae*)	185
Whites & Sulphurs (*Pieridae*)	173	Tiger Moths (*Arctiidae*)	186
Coppers, Hairstreaks (*Lycaenidae*)	174	Prominents (*Notodontidae*)	188
Brush-footed Butterflies (*Nymphalidae*)	177	Tent Caterpillars (*Lasiocampidae*)	189
Skippers (*Hesperidae*)	180	Owlet Moths (*Noctuidae*)	190
Sphinx Moths (*Sphingidae*)	181	Clearwing Moths (*Sesiidae*)	191
Giant Silkworm Moths (*Saturniidae*)	182	Plume Moths (*Pterophoridae*)	191
Inchworms, Geometers (*Geometridae*)	184		

Scorpionflies (Mecoptera)   192–195

Common Scorpionflies (*Panorpidae*)   194
Snow Scorpionflies (*Boreidae*)   195

True Flies (Diptera)   196–233

Crane Flies (*Tipulidae*)	198	Flower Flies (*Syrphidae*)	218
Phantom Crane Flies (*Ptychopteridae*)	200	Dung Flies (*Scathophagidae*)	221
Winter Crane Flies (*Trichoceridae*)	201	Muscid Flies (*Muscidae*)	222
Black Flies (*Simulidae*)	202	Root-maggot Flies (*Anthomyiidae*)	223
Mosquitoes (*Culicidae*)	203	Blow Flies (*Calliphoridae*)	224
March Flies (*Bibionidae*)	204	Flesh Flies (*Sarcophagidae*)	225
Dark-winged Fungus Gnats (*Sciaridae*)	204	Parasitic Flies (*Tachinidae*)	226
Midges (*Chironomidae*)	205	Fruit Flies (*Tephritidae*)	228
Horse Flies, Deer Flies (*Tabanidae*)	206	Picture-winged Flies (*Ulidiidae*)	230
Snipe Flies (*Rhagionidae*)	208	Signal Flies (*Platystomatidae*)	230
Soldier Flies (*Stratiomyidae*)	209	Grass Flies (Frit Flies) (*Chloropidae*)	231
Robber Flies (*Asilidae*)	210	Stilt-legged Flies (*Micropezidae*)	232
Bee Flies (*Bombylidae*)	214	Black Scavenger Flies (*Sepsidae*)	233
Long-legged Flies (*Dolichopodidae*)	216		

Glossary   **234**
Insect Websites   **236**
Photo Credits   **236**
Titles of Interest   **237**
Index   **238**

Dedicated to

Jim Demler,

You helped fuel the two passions that I have in my life—insects and running. I would not be where I am today without your mentoring, guidance and encouragement.

Acknowledgements

I would first like to thank Mark Sparky Stensaas for the opportunity to write and illustrate this book. When he first approached me to consider this project, I was very excited for the chance to write it. Writing a book is something many of us dream about and I appreciate the opportunity to make this one a reality. I would also like to thank Rick Kollath for his excellent graphics. I would also like to express my gratitude to Janet Moe for her help in scanning my many slides.

This book would not be possible without the help of some of my colleagues. I particularly want to thank John Luhman, Ralph Holzenthal, Dan Hansen, and Amanda Roe for their help in identifying images, reviewing chapters, and general counsel. Your expertise and willingness to help me in this project are greatly appreciated.

I would like to especially thank James "Ding" Johnson. He not only provided me help for my book but he was one of my committee advisors when I was in graduate school. He taught me much about insects, especially in several taxonomy classes, as well as help guide me through my Master's program. Ding has always been a source of encouragement through the years.

I would also like to thank the following colleagues and fellow entomologists for their help in identifying images or reviewing chapters for this book: Michael Ackland, Gary Anweiler, Roger Blahnik, Scott Brooks, Phil Clausen, Jason Dombroskie, Elaine Evans, Len Ferrington, Jon Gelhaus, Jon Haarstad, Dean Hansen, Ron Huber, Boris Kondratieff, Lloyd Knutson, Jean-François Landry, Jay McPherson, Roger Moon, Riley Nelson, Phil Pellitteri, John Polhemus, Greg Setliff, Marla Spivak, Susan Weller, and Jennifer Zaspel.

And finally I would like to thank my partner Leila for her patience and understanding in the many hours I devoted to working on this book over the last several years. Thank you for letting me follow this dream.

Jeffrey Hahn
July 21, 2009

We at Kollath-Stensaas are very excited about this book. It fills a gap in the local field guides that has been too long in coming. Jeffrey had a monumental task in preparing the species list and text, but he did a wonderful job. Also note that many of the beautiful photographs are his; insects are not easy to photograph! The publishers would like to thank Eric Eaton for his expertise in reviewing parts of the text. Enjoy!

The publishers
July 23, 2009

Insect Parts

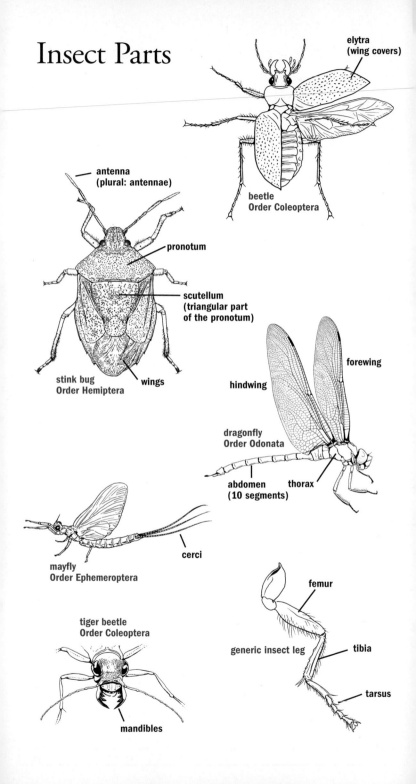

elytra
(wing covers)

beetle
Order Coleoptera

antenna
(plural: antennae)

pronotum

scutellum
(triangular part
of the pronotum)

stink bug
Order Hemiptera

wings

forewing

hindwing

dragonfly
Order Odonata

abdomen
(10 segments)

thorax

cerci

mayfly
Order Ephemeroptera

tiger beetle
Order Coleoptera

femur

generic insect leg

tibia

tarsus

mandibles

Success

Insects are the most numerous and successful animals on earth. Entomologists have identified about 90,000 different species living in North America and about one million different species in the world. In a typical backyard, there can be as many as 1,000 different insects at any given time. They are successful for several reasons. First, insects occupy essentially all types of habitats except for oceans, using many resources as food. These resources can be divided into three general groups: herbivores, i.e. feeding on plants, carnivores, i.e. feeding on insects and other animals, and saprivores, i.e. feeding on dead or decaying plant or animal material. Insects are also successful because of their small size, their adaptability and their high reproductive rate. As a consequence, there are three times the number of insects compared to all other terrestrial animals in North America combined.

What is an Insect?

Insects belong to a group of animals called arthropods. Arthropods possess segmented bodies, a hard external integument known as an exoskeleton and paired jointed appendages, e.g. legs and antennae. In addition to insects, other common arthropods include arachnids (e.g. ticks, spiders, daddylong-legs, mites), crustaceans (e.g. crayfish, sowbugs, fairyshrimp), millipedes and centipedes.

Insects differ from these other arthropods by possessing three major body parts, the head, thorax and abdomen.

Several important features are found on the head. There is one pair of antennae found on the adult's head, usually found between or in front of the eyes. Antennae vary in form and complexity, and are sometimes referred to as feelers or horns. Antennae are used by insects for many types of sensing, including smelling, hearing, tasting and feeling. Insects also possess compound eyes which are made up of varying numbers of facets. Each facet sees a small part of what the insect is viewing. Together, they comprise what the insect sees. The number of facets in a compound eye varies from as few as several facets as in some subterranean ants and many as 50,000 facets in the large eyes of dragonflies.

Look for insect mouthparts on the head. They are mandibulate, i.e. possessing mandibles, although there is much variation. Mouthparts can be generally divided up into two types: chewing mouthparts, i.e. mandibles (jaws) are prominent, or sucking mouthparts, i.e. the mouthparts are modified into beak-like or tube-like mouthparts. While they differ considerably in appearance, the same basic parts are found in both types.

The second major body part is the thorax. It is divided into three sections, prothorax, mesothorax and metathorax. There is a pair of legs on each thoracic segment, a total of six (a few adult insects possess no legs). Legs vary much in form and function. Legs are used for running and walking, jumping, grasping, swimming and digging. The wings are also attached to the thorax. Most insects have four wings, attached to the second and third thoracic segments (mesothorax and metathorax). Flies have only two wings which are attached to the mesothorax). A few insects lack wings altogether. The wings exhibit a wide variety of modifications.

The last major insect body part is the abdomen which generally possesses eleven segments and usually lacks appendages. The abdomen is relatively simple in structure compared to the head and thorax. Some insects possess a pair of appendages on the last segment of the abdomen known as cerci. Cerci vary in form and usually function as sensory organs. Females typically possess claspers and ovipositors on the abdomen for mating and laying eggs. Some insects, such as bees and wasps, possess a stinger on the abdomen which is a modified ovipositor.

Metamorphosis: Insect Development

Insects are generally oviparous, i.e. they lay eggs. Eggs are generally oval and elongate, although there can be much variation. Eggs can be laid singly or in clusters. Many insects surround their eggs in some sort of protective material. A few insects, e.g. aphids, are viviparous, i.e. eggs develop inside the mother and she gives birth to live young.

Because their hard outer integument does not expand, immature insects must shed their exoskeletons through a process called molting. The stage of the insect between molts is called an instar. Insects often have four or five instars, although this varies with different insect species.

Insects develop through a phenomenon called metamorphosis. Metamorphosis is a change in form during development. Sometimes this change is gradual but many times it is very dramatic. Insect development is broadly divided into two different types, simple and complete metamorphosis.

The life stages of simple metamorphosis are egg, nymph, adult. The immature nymphs look similar to the adults except nymphs are smaller, lack wings and are sexually immature. Their wings develop on the outside of their bodies. The last nymphal instar molts into an adult. There are three types of simple metamorphosis: ametabolous where the adults are wingless and the only difference between nymphs and adults is size, hemimetabolous, where the nymphs (sometimes called naiads) are aquatic differ considerably in form from the adults which live on land

and paurometabolous where the nymphs and adults are similar in form, differing chiefly in size, and typically live the same environment.

The life stages for complete metamorphosis, also called holometabolous, are egg, larva, pupa and adult. Larvae look very different from adults, usually feeding on different types of food and living in different habitats. Last instar larvae molt into a pupa or resting stage. In the pupal stage, the insect does not feed and usually does not move. Inside the pupa, the insect changes form through tissue breakdown, tissue reorganization and the development of new structures, such as wings, legs, antennae and mouthparts from masses of specialized cells. Wings develop inside the body. The insect eventually molts one last time with the adult insect emerging from the pupa.

How to Enjoy Insects

The great thing about insects is that they occur essentially everywhere in the north woods. Although they are most common during warm weather, you can find them nearly at all of times of the year. When I am hiking, I like to look on all kinds of plants, especially on the flowers and leaves. Be also sure to examine stems, bark and branches. Don't forget most insects like to be in the warmth and you can often find them sunning themselves in a variety of areas.

Insects are frequently found on the ground, either as they scurry about or are resting after flight. Some insects nest in the soil and you may find them as they are leaving or returning to it. If you encounter logs, give them a good look, especially under any loose bark. It is also worth looking under logs, as well as any loose stones, or similar objects. When my son Chris was young, we had a rock in the backyard we would lift most evenings to see what small critters were hiding underneath (of course we always placed it exactly where we found it so we could try again another day). If you aren't too squeamish, check out dead animals and dung, there is an amazing array of insects that are attracted to these food sources.

Don't forget sources of water, including ponds, lakes, streams, rivers, marshes, bogs for the many species of aquatic insects. Be sure to also check out shorelines for semi-aquatic insects. The immatures of many insects are aquatic and as adults they are found nearby on land on plants and other objects.

Insects are common in and around buildings. Many of these enter inadvertently but there are some species that have adapted to living with people quite nicely.

Getting Closer

If you want to be more proactive in finding insects and observing them up close, you can use different capture methods. One common type, known as sweeping, is done by moving a heavy duty net back and forth through tall plants. This collects a variety of small insects that may otherwise be overlooked.

Another common collecting method is pit fall traps. Sink a tin can or similar container into the ground so the top is even with the ground. Insects walking on the ground fall into the container and become trapped. Drill a small hole into the bottom to prevent water from accumulating. Place a piece of old fruit or other type of material as bait to attract insects. Different baits attract different insects. Place a fine-meshed screen over the bait to make it easier to remove insects that fall into it.

Also check outdoor lights at night which attract a wide variety of different insects.

Black (UV) lights are the most attractive. Not all nocturnal insects may be attracted to lights so inspect plants and other nearby sites at night.

You can spend many enjoyable hours watching insects, observing their habits and behavior. You do not need any special equipment to watch them. You can get close to many insects with a slow stealthy approach and practice. If you are fortunate enough to have a device that magnifies images, such as a pair of binoculars that can focus to within six to eight feet, you can increase the number and variety of insects you can observe without the need to get as close.

You will be able to identify many insects to order and even family from your observations and with the common and familiar insects, to species. If you encounter an insect you can not immediately identify, capture it with a jar or insect net so you can examine it more closely without it being able to escape. You can then release the insect after you have an opportunity to look at it more thoroughly.

Photography

One way to take your insect watching a step further is to photograph them. The technological advances with digital photography enables people to buy cameras and shoot pictures for a reasonable amount of money. You can shoot with a point and shoot camera, using the macro or close up setting, although this is usually better suited for larger insects and less so for smaller ones. You may also want to investigate using a subcompact internally focusing, fixed lens camera. The lens focuses inside the cameras (as opposed to an point and shoot camera lens extending out). This can give you reasonably good shots for many insects.

If you intend to get more serious with your insect photography, you will want to use an single lens reflex (SLR) camera, i.e. one that uses interchangeable lens, along with a true macro lens (e.g. I have a Vivitar 100mm macro on my old film SLR camera and a Tamron 180mm macro on my digital camera). To be able get sufficient depth of field, you will need to use a flash. This should be mounted on a bracket off of the camera as a flash mounted in the hot shoe will not illuminate the insects you are shooting. You are so close to your subject that you can not get the flash to point down enough at the subject.

Collecting

Of course, the activity many people associate with insects is collecting them. This is an activity for people of all ages. Children especially like to collect insects, I was no exception.

You don't need much equipment to collect insects. You need something to catch them with, like a jar or insect net. You should also have a pair of forceps for handling insects, a spreading board and pinning block insect pins and a storage box. You should be able to purchase these items from hobby shops or biological supply companies.

Once you have captured an insect, you will need to kill it so it can be pinned. The easiest way is to put the insect into a freezer for a day or two. As long as the jar is air tight, the insects will stay relaxed until you are ready to remove them from the freezer and are ready to pin them.

You can also make a killing jar by using a wide-mouth glass jar with a tightly fitting screw lid. Place an absorbent material like cotton or cut up rubber bands on the bottom and apply ethyl acetate (fingernail polish remover) to it. Cut out a piece of cardboard in a circle to tightly fit into the jar. Recharge when necessary. You should pin insects soon after they are killed before they have a chance to become rigid.

Spreading boards are useful for laying the wings of insects out flat and holding them in place while the specimen dries. They can be bought at a biological supply company. A pinning block can be any piece of styrofoam (styrofoam used for packing appliances in boxes, for instance). A pinning block is useful to position legs and other body parts before the insect dries. A pinning block can also be used as a mounting board by cutting a rectangular slit large enough to position an insect's body and allow the wings to lay flat. Different-sized slits are necessary for different-sized insects.

Use insect pins for pinning the insects. Insect pins are long, slender pins made specifically for mounting insects. They are available from a biological supply company. Size #2 and #3 are the most useful for general collectors.

You should record information about the specimen on labels. Labels for pinned specimens should be made on relatively heavy stock paper (about 120 pound). You can purchase blank labels from a biological supply company or you can make your own with unlined index cards or heavy paper. Each label should be approximately 1/2 x 3/4 inch in size or smaller. For neatness, all labels should be close to the same size.

You should include information about where you collected the insect (nearest town, county and state), the date the specimen was collected (day, month and year), name of the collector, any specific information about where the insect was collected (e.g. feeding on oak leaf, on goldenrod flower, collected at black light etc.).

You can store your insect collection in Schmidt boxes or similar insect storage boxes available at biological supply companies. Cigar boxes and small cardboard boxes may be used but only for short-term storage as carpet beetles and other scavenging insects can get into these boxes and destroy specimens. Cut out a piece of corrugated cardboard or styrofoam the same size as the bottom of the box to make it easier to place the specimens in the box. Larger collections can be stored in glass-topped display cases. Display cases can be bought from a biological supply company or constructed at home

Rest the specimen on a pinning block and steady the insect by holding it in place with a forceps. Place the insect pin into the insect body. Insects are generally pinned through the thorax on the right side. Approximately 3/8 inch of the pin should be showing above the insect body, enough so you can comfortably hold the pin with little risk of accidentally touching the specimen

Once the insect is pinned you can spread the wings by placing it on the spreading board so the wings are level with the top of the board. Position the wings where you want them, then use strips of paper anchored by pins to hold the wings down. If it is necessary to position any body parts, place the specimen on a pinning block and use insect pins to maneuver the body part into the position you want. Leave specimens for at least several days to a week to allow them to dry.

How to use this Field Guide

Insects of the North Woods is designed to make field identification easier for you, the reader. We have made this possible through the use of color-coded tabs, size bars and over 600 color photos. Also, by limiting the insects to those found in one geographic area, we have eliminated the need to wade through many hundreds of species, many of which would never be found here.

This book focuses on Minnesota, Wisconsin, Michigan and northwest Ontario. But remember, not all species are found in any single area. Habitat preferences tend to spread species out. The North Woods is a mosaic of different habitats from bogs, oak woods, sand dunes and grasslands to lakes, ponds, marshes and rivers; and about everything in between.

Coverage

With tens of thousands of insect species in the North Woods, we could obviously not include all, or even most. Nor would we want to. Only the most common, the most interesting, the really bizarre and the vividly colored made the cut. The author sought to give you, the reader, a broad overview of the insect families that one might encounter in the field. We purposefully left out the urban/household critters that are restricted to those environs. For example, you will not find head lice nor house cockroaches in this book.

Order

Insects are organized by order and then broken down further into families and genera. We attempted to put closely related species together to further simplify identification. Family name is listed at the bottom of each spread. With experience in the field using this guide, you will gradually learn to identify insect orders and even place the insects you see, collect or photograph into their proper family or even genus.

Insect Names

Like other organisms, insects are given a scientific name. The Latin names tend to be the spoken word of entomologists. The insects with widely accepted common name are few; in cases where there is no common name we simply use the name for that group. For example, the fly *Laphria canis* has no common name so we call it by the group it belongs to, "robber fly." We capitalize species names but use lower case for groups (e.g. Six-spotted Tiger Beetles are actually a type of beetle).

Photos

We chose to use photos of free-flying insects in their natural habitat. Most images were provided by the author and the publisher, but we acquired other images from several different dedicated and talented photographers. Photographing insects is not an easy task! We attempted to use photos that illustrated the best field marks. Sexual dimorphism (different coloration or shape in males and females) is the norm for some species; we label the photos as male or female in cases where it may aid in identification.

Size Scale

Size is relative and often hard to judge in the field. Use the size-bars overlain each species' photo. The black bar indicates the actual body length of that species, except in the case of the butterflies and moths where it depicts average wingspan.

Enjoy *Insects of the North Woods*. Take it in the field. Cram it in your pack. Use it. But most importantly, have fun getting to know our fascinating northern insects.

Introductory text for every Order and Family covered

Different header colors are used to quickly access species in that insect Order

Species text covers identification tips, behavior, life cycle, natural history and phenology

Color tabs identify which insect order the critter belongs. It also helps you flip to the right section

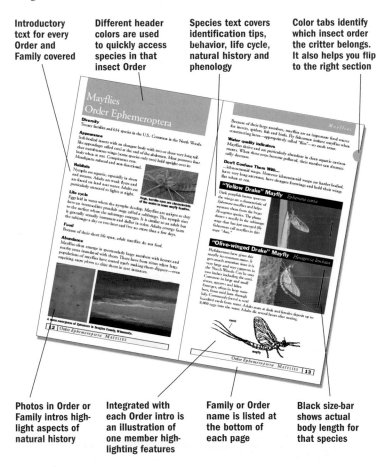

Photos in Order or Family intros highlight aspects of natural history

Integrated with each Order intro is an illustration of one member highlighting features

Family or Order name is listed at the bottom of each page

Black size-bar shows actual body length for that species

Springtails
Order Collembola

Diversity
There are 12 families and 795 species in North America. Springtails are very common in the North Woods.

Appearance
Adults: Very small insects, ranging in size from $1/16^{th}$ to $1/8^{th}$ inch long. These wingless insects are usually elongate shaped, although some, like sminthurid springtails, are round and stout. Springtails have short to moderate length antennae with mouthparts generally concealed inside their head and not noticed. Most springtails are dark-colored, brown, gray or black although some species are also white, and some are even iridescent and brightly colored.

Most springtails possess a furcula located on the underside of the abdomen—a few springtails lack such an appendage. A furcula is a forked appendage used for jumping. When not in use, a furcula is tucked up under the body, set like a mouse trap. When it is released, it extends down rapidly propelling the springtail forward. A springtail can jump many times its body length.

Immatures: Very similar to adults but are smaller.

Habitats
Springtails are associated with damp conditions and are commonly found in the soil and leaf litter. They are also common under bark, decaying wood, and in fungi. At least one species is common in freshwater ponds, even puddles. Another species is common on top of snow during winter and early spring. You can occasionally find springtails indoors in damp areas like showers, bathtubs and potted plants.

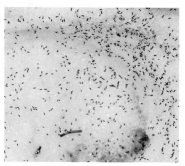

Some springtails are very common on top of the snow on warm winter days. They are known as "snow fleas."

Life Cycle
Springtails develop using ametabolous metamorphosis, a type of simple metamorphosis.

springtail

Food

They feed on fungi and decaying plant matter. A few are predaceous on very small invertebrate animals.

Abundance

Despite their small size, springtails can occur in tremendously large numbers and are one of the most abundant insects. One source estimates that millions of springtails occur per hectare (about 2.5 acres).

Regenerating lost body parts

Springtails have the ability to regenerate antennae which are frequently damaged or lost due to attacks by ground beetles and other predaceous insects.

Don't confuse them with...

...fleas. Because they are small and jump, people sometimes misidentify springtails with fleas. However, fleas are flattened from side to side while springtails are cylindrical in shape. You would not commonly see fleas in soil, leaf litter, or other places where you would expect springtails.

Snow Flea *Hypogastrura nivicola*

Snow fleas have a higher tolerance for colder temperatures than most insects and are often found in large numbers ON TOP of the snow! Hibernating in soil during winter, they become active as the weather warms and the snow starts to melt. They are able to move up through breaks in the snow to reach the surface; Sometimes massing in such large numbers that they literally turn the snow black. Watch for snow fleas especially around the bases of trees. They feed on microscopic fungi, algae and decaying organic matter.

Mayflies
Order Ephemeroptera

Diversity
Twenty families and 614 species in the U.S.. Common in the North Woods.

Appearance
Soft-bodied insects with an elongate body with two or three very long tail-like appendages called cerci at the end of the abdomen. Most possesses four clear membranous wings (some species only two) held upright over its body when at rest. Conspicuous eyes. Mouthparts reduced and non-functional.

Habitats
Nymphs are aquatic, especially in rivers and streams. Adults are weak flyers and are found on land near water. Adults are particularly attracted to lights at night.

Huge, hat-like eyes are characteristic of the males in some mayfly families.

Life cycle
Mayflies develop using hemimetabolous metamorphosis, a type of simple of metamorphosis. Eggs laid in water where the nymphs develop. Mayflies are unique as they have an intermediate preadult stage called a subimago. It is similar to an adult but is generally sexually immature and duller in color. Adults emerge from the subimago a day or two later and live no more than a few days.

Food
Because of their short life span, adult mayflies do not feed.

Abundance
Mayflies often emerge in spectacularly large numbers with homes and nearby areas inundated with them. There have been times when large populations of mayflies have coated roads making them slippery—even requiring snow plows to clear them in rare instances.

A mass emergence of *Ephemera* in Douglas County, Minnesota.

Because of their large numbers, mayflies are an important food source for insects, spiders, fish and birds. Fly fishermen imitate mayflies when constructing lures—appropriately called "flies"—to catch trout.

Water quality indicators

Mayflies thrive and are particularly abundant in clean aquatic environments. When these areas become polluted, their number can dramatically decrease.

Don't Confuse Them With...

...ichneumonid wasps. However ichneumonid wasps are harder bodied, have very long antennae, have elongate forewings and hold their wings flat when at rest.

"Olive-winged Drake" Mayfly *Hexagenia limbata*

Flyfishermen have given this mayfly its common name. It gets much attention since it is very large and very common in the North Woods. Can be over two inches including the cerci. Common in large and small rivers, streams and lakes. Emerges, often in large numbers, from mid June through July. Commonly found several hundred yards from water. Adults mate at dusk and females deposit up to 8,000 eggs into the water. Adults die several hours after mating.

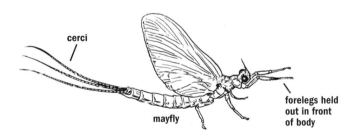

cerci

mayfly

forelegs held out in front of body

Dragonflies & Damselflies
Order Odonata

Diversity

There are 11 families and 434 species in the United States. Dragonflies and damselflies are very common in the North Woods.

Appearance

Adults: Medium to large insects with four conspicuous wings containing many veins. They have large compound eyes and long, slender abdomens. The Odonata are divided into two suborders, the Anisoptera, the dragonflies and the Zygoptera, the damselflies. Dragonflies hold their wings straight out at rest. The two pairs of wings are similar in length although the hind pair is wider at the base. The compound eyes touch or are separated by a distance shorter than the width of one compound eye. Damselflies hold their wings over their back when they are rest. Both pairs of wings are the same size and are narrowed at the base. The compound eyes are separated by width greater than one compound eye.

Larvae: The immature nymphs (sometimes called naiads) are generally cylindrical and streamlined. Dragonfly nymphs are generally more stout than damselfly nymphs. Damselfly nymphs have three leaf-like gills at the tip of their abdomen while dragonfly nymphs possess inconspicuous gills that are not noticed. The mouthparts are modified into arm-like structures which they keep folded under their head when not in use. They extend these mouthparts forward when they attempt to capture food.

Habitats

The nymphs are aquatic. Adults are often found near water where they nymphs develop but can wander far from any water source.

Biology

Dragonflies and damselflies develop using hemimetabolous metamorphosis, a type of simple metamorphosis. Both adults and nymphs are predaceous feeding primarily on insects. Adults prey on a variety of flying insects. The nymphs feed on a variety of aquatic insects including mayfly nymphs although larger dragonfly nymphs have been known to attack tadpoles and small fish.

Don't confuse them with...

...Nerve-winged insects like lacewings, dobsonflies, and related insects can look similar to damselflies. Nerve-winged insects have longer antennae and they usually hold their wings tent-like. Dragonfly and damselfly nymphs could be confused with mayfly and stonefly nymphs although these insects have conspicuous gills on the thorax (stonefly nymphs) or abdomen (mayfly nymphs).

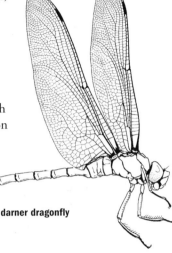

darner dragonfly

Further your knowledge

In a book of this scope we can only cover so many species. If you want to delve deeper into the world of the "odes," pick up a copy of Kollath-Stensaas's comprehensive field guides to the dragonflies of the North Woods. All species have range maps and phenograms.

A guide to all 102 North Woods dragonflies by Minnesota biologist Kurt Mead. *Dragonflies of the North Woods: 2nd Edition* ISBN: 978-0-9792006-5-6

Darners
Family Aeshnidae

Appearance

Darners are usually between 2 ³/8 to 3 ¹/8 inches long. Their compound eyes touch considerably on top. They usually are brownish with green and blue, sometimes yellow markings on the thorax and abdomen. Their wings are clear.

Biology

Darners have a well-developed ovipositor and lay their eggs in plant stems along the edges of lakes and ponds, and uncommonly around streams. Typically the female lays her eggs without a male guarding her. Darners are present from May to October.

Common Green Darner *Anax junius*

Famous for its long distance migrations from the northern U.S. to Texas and other southern states. Tens of thousands can be seen moving south down the North Shore of Lake Superior in the fall. Their offspring return in spring and are the first dragonflies we see in the North. Ranges from 2⁵/8 to 3¹/8 inches in length. It has a green thorax and either a blue abdomen (males) or a purplish gray one (females). It has a distinctive black and yellow bullseye pattern on top of its head in front of the eyes. It is typically found near still water, especially ponds and marshes. April to October.

Canada Darner *Aeshna canadensis*

Probably the most common "blue darner" (*Aeshna* genus) in the North Woods. Look for the deeply cleft front thoracic shoulder stripe; the notch is at a 90 degree angle which separates this species from the Lake Darner (less than 90 degrees) and Green-striped Darner (greater than 90 degrees). Averages 2³/4 inch long. Look for them around sluggish streams, beaver ponds and lakes with boggy or marshy edges.

Clubtails
Family Gomphidae

Appearance

Clubtails range in size from 1 5/8 to 3 1/3 inches in length. Unlike other dragonflies, their compound eyes do not touch on top. Their wings are clear and the posterior segments of the abdomen of most clubtails are enlarged. Clubtails are usually green or yellow with black markings and have clear wings.

Biology

Clubtails mate for a few minutes before the female goes off to lay eggs; the male does not go with to guard her. Clubtails have an undeveloped ovipositor and they drop their eggs into flowing water and less commonly along the edges of ponds and lakes. Clubtails often like to rest on the ground and other flat surfaces, although they can also be found on foliage. They are present from May to September.

Dragonhunter *Hagenius brevistylus*

Among "dragonflyers," this is probably the most sought after species in the North Woods. It is very large, averaging 3 1/3 inches in length, and can take large prey such as Monarchs and other dragonflies (hence, the common name). It is immune to Monarch toxins and the effects of wasp stings. Usually found near flowing rivers, rapids but also rocky northern lakeshores and even bogs. June to August.

Black-shouldered Spinyleg *Dromogomphus spinosus*

The common name highlights the two most important field marks to look for on this species; the wide black shoulder stripe and the large spines on the hind leg. Averages 2 1/2 inches long. Adults fade from bright yellow to blue as they age. Watch for this large clubtail along streams, rivers and lakes with rocky shorelines. June into September.

Emeralds
Family Corduliidae

Appearance

Moderate sized dragonflies, 1¼ to 3¼ inches long. They are usually blackish or brown with some species being metallic green. Emeralds have brilliantly colored green eyes and usually have markings on the wings

Biology

They are typically associated with ponds, wooded streams, and bogs. These dragonflies common from May into August.

American Emerald *Cordulia shurtleffii*

A very common emerald of wooded areas. They almost always perch vertically by hanging from branches (as in photo). Males have a wide clubbed abdomen. Look for the pale ring around the base of the abdomen. Eggs are laid in boggy ponds, sedge marshes and lakes. 1 ¾ inches. Late May through July.

Racket-tailed Emerald *Dorocordulia libera*

Similar to the American Emerald but note the yellow triangular band around the base of the abdomen. Larvae develop in the acidic waters of marsh-edged ponds, lakes and sluggish rivers. Averages 1 ⅝ inches long. Adults fly early June to mid August.

Common Baskettail *Epitheca cynosura*

Massive emergences of Common Baskettails can fill the air with dragonflies in late May and early June. Their hind wings usually have dark patches at their base; this feature helps separate them from the very similar Beaverpond and Spiny Baskettails. Breed near lakes, rivers and ponds with marshy edges and mucky bottoms. Late May to mid July.

Skimmers
Family Libellulidae

Appearance

Skimmers typically range in size from 1 to 2 inches in length. Their eyes touch on top. Veins in the hindwings form a boot-shape. The wings may be clear but often has spots or bands. They vary in color with combinations including brown, red, black, white, yellow, and blue.

Biology

Skimmers are associated with ponds and swamps where they are commonly found perching nearby on twigs, grass, and similar objects. Mating takes place while in flight. Females dip their abdomens into the water when they lay eggs while males guard them. Skimmers are common from May to October.

Four-spotted Skimmer   *Libellula quadrimaculata*

Four-spotted Skimmers can be abundant at times. They are also easy to observe as they often hunt over land and perch frequently at the tips of shrub branches, often at eye level. Note especially the two black spots on each wing, the dark triangles at the base of the hindwing and the amber leading edge to the wings. Mid May to late August.

Twelve-spotted Skimmer   *Libellula pulchella*

One of our most stunning dragonflies; twelve black spots and ten white spots grace the wings (sometimes called Ten-spot Skimmer). Averages 2 inches long. Its abdomen is brown with either yellow spots along the sides (male) or a yellow stripe (females). Like most dragonflies, it can be seen in many habitats other than its breeding habitat (which in the is case is rivers, ponds and lakes with marshy edges. Flies late May through September.

Common Whitetail *Plathemis (Libellula) lydia*

You can't mistake adult males of this species! The wide and fat abdomen is chalk white (actually pruinose) and the wings are marked with large black patches. Females and young males have a brown abdomen edged with white triangles. They normally perch low, on ground or on rocks. Late May to early September.

Widow Skimmer *Libellula luctuosa*

The male's very distinctive wing pattern makes field identification easy; large black wing patches are edged laterally by broad white wing stripes (almost appearing blue in some cases). Immature males and females lack the white wing bands and have a black and orange abdomen. May to August.

Chalk-fronted Corporal *Ladona julia*

Named for the two white "officer stripes" on the top front of the thorax, the corporals can fly in numbers that seem to be an army. This is a gregarious species, often congregating in large numbers along logging roads, boat docks and along wooded trails. Adults fly late May until early August.

White-faced Meadowhawk *Sympetrum obtrusum*

The bright white face of this meadowhawk makes identification easy in a notoriously difficult group. Deep red abdomen edged with black triangles. The orange juveniles are impossible to separate in the field from other juvenile meadowhawks. Adults forage in forest openings. Mid June to late October.

Autumn Meadowhawk *Sympetrum vicinum*

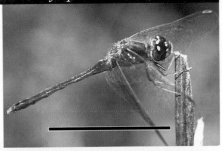

The bright white face of this meadowhawk makes identification easy in a notoriously difficult group. Deep red abdomen edged with black triangles. The orange juveniles are impossible to separate in the field from other juvenile meadowhawks. Adults forage in forest openings. Mid June to late October.

Common Pondhawk *Erythemis simplicicollis*

Shown in the photo is the female; the male is powdery blue with a green face, green eyes and white claspers. Hunts around ponds, ferociously darting out from its perch to grab anything its size or smaller—even other pondhawks! Formerly called the Eastern Pondhawk.

Dot-tailed Whiteface *Leucorrhinia intacta*

The front of its head is white and its body is black with a squarish yellow dot on the abdomen near the tip. A recently emerged dot-tailed whiteface has more yellow on its abdomen and thorax. Its wings are usually clear. One of the first dragonflies to emerge in spring; on the wing from mid May to September.

Calico Pennant *Celithemis elisa*

Red "hearts" adorn the top of the male's black abdomen. Both male and female sport red wing spots. Females have a similar pattern but with yellow abdominal spots. While hunting in fields, marshes or lakeshores, they often perch horizontally at the tip of rushes or small branches. Late May into August.

Damselflies
Suborder Zygoptera

Closely related to dragonflies are the delicate damselflies (suborder Zygoptera). Damsels differ in wing shape (all four wings the same size and shape), resting posture (wings held up over their back—except in the *Lestes* spreadwings), separate eyes, a functional ovipositor and weak, fluttery flight.

River Jewelwing *Calopteryx aequabilis*

When this iridescent emerald beauty with black tipped wings flutters by your canoe, you're sure to take notice. Males can be seen hunting and squabbling over territory along quiet streams or fast-flowing rivers. The female has an iridescent bronze body, smoky wings with a white spot at the tip. The similar Ebony Jewelwing has all black wings.

Slender Spreadwing *Lestes rectangularis*

A damselfly perched with its wings spread is sure to be a member of the spreadwing family (Lestidae). The male has an abdomen twice as long as its wings. It overwinters in the egg stage. Look for hunting spreadwings in emergent rushes or the marshy edges of lakes and ponds from June into September.

Familiar Bluet *Enallagma civile*

There are many species of bluets but the most common is the aptly named Familiar Bluet. Their abdomen is mostly blue with only narrow black markings. Females are generally less colorful, and are typically green, yellow-green, or tan. Bluets are common from late May to early September.

Stoneflies
Order Plecoptera

Diversity
There are nine families and 537 species in the United States. Stoneflies are common in the North Woods.

Appearance
Adults: Small to medium sized insects, usually dark-colored, although some, especially spring or summer emerging stoneflies, may be yellowish or greenish. They possess four thin membranous wings containing many veins. The wings are held flat over their backs when at rest, extending a little past the tip of their abdomens. The first pair is a little longer and more narrower than the broader somewhat shorter hind wings. At least a few winter stoneflies, like *Allocapnia*, have very shortened wings. Stoneflies possess moderately long antennae and chewing mouthparts, although in many species the mouthparts are reduced. Stoneflies also have a pair of cerci on the ends of their abdomens.

Nymphs: Nymphs are similar in form to adults except they lack wings. They possess small, inconspicuous gills on their thorax and two long cerci on the tips of their abdomens. They also have two pairs of tarsal claws.

Large nymphs of the family Perlidae (Common Stoneflies) are beautifully patterned. This is *Acroneuria carolinensis*.

Habitats
Stonefly nymphs are aquatic and are typically found under stones in clean, unpolluted, highly oxygenated water, particularly streams as well as along river and lake shores. Adult stoneflies are poor flyers and are generally found near water.

Life Cycle
Stoneflies develop using hemimetabolous metamorphosis, a type of simple metamorphosis. Many stoneflies are active during spring and

Adults of some species emerge in late winter. This is a *Taeniopteryx* species on snow.

summer, although there are a lot of species that are active during fall and winter (sometimes referred to as winter stoneflies).

When a male is looking for a female to mate with, it drums with its abdomen on a surface, such as a log or tree branch. This sends vibrations to which interested females can respond. The specific rhythms of these mating drums are specific to a particular species.

Once mated, females lay eggs on the water surface which sink to the bottom. The nymphs hatch and spend their entire lives in the water. When nymphs are fully developed, they crawl out of the water to emerge as adults. Many species complete their development within one year although there are others that may take several years.

Food
Winter stonefly nymphs generally feed on submerged plant matter and organic debris, while summer stonefly nymphs are usually predaceous on small aquatic organisms, such as midge larvae. Adult winter stoneflies generally feed on algae, lichens, pollen, and fungal hyphae and spores while summer stoneflies typically don't feed.

Water Quality Indicators
Because they prefer clean bodies of waters with a high level of oxygen, stoneflies are good indicators of water quality.

Don't confuse them with...
...mayfly nymphs. Stonefly nymphs are easily confused with mayfly nymphs. Mayfly nymphs, however, possess three caudal filaments, i.e. tails, have obvious gills on their abdomen, and have only one tarsal claw.

Adult stoneflies may be confused with mayflies, caddisflies, or alderflies, dobsonflies, and similar insects. However mayflies hold their triangular wings straight up over their back and possess very short antennae. Caddisflies have very long antennae, lack cerci on the abdomen, and possess hairy wings held tent-like over the body. Alderflies, dobsonflies, and similar insects lack cerci and hold their wings tent-like over their bodies.

stonefly nymph

Spinyleg Willowfly *Taeniopteryx species*

Spinyleg willowflies are a type of winter stonefly. Adults are dark. Nymphs are yellowish brown with a white stripe down their backs. Like other winter stoneflies, the nymphs feed on organic material in the water. This stonefly is usually associated with large rivers, like the Mississippi, as well as smaller rivers and streams. Adults commonly emerge in March and April, although they can be seen as early as January and February.

Giant Stonefly *Pteronarcys species*

There is a reason these insects are in the Giant Stonefly family; Larvae may reach two inches in length and adults may be $1^1/_2$ inches long including the wings. Two species are found in the North Woods, *Pteronarcy dorsata*, American Salmonfly and *P. pictetii*, Midwestern Salmonfly. These two species are the largest stoneflies in the North Woods. Nymphs are found in medium and large streams, especially amongst fast water where organic material accumulates. Nymphs feed on decaying plant matter, including leaves, diatoms and are also occasionally predaceous. It takes three years for these stoneflies to complete their life cycle. Adults emerge in April and May.

Snowfly (Small Winter Stonefly) *Allocapnia species*

Wander along the snowy banks of a clear running river on a warmer winter day—usually in late February, March or early April—and you will likely see some small elongate black insects wandering across the snow. Now look closer, they have two "tails" (cerci) coming out of the end of the abdomen. They don't fly but rather walk about feeding on algae. They can be active down to 20 degrees F.

Grasshoppers, Katydids & Crickets
Order Orthoptera

Diversity
There are 16 families and 1145 species in the United States. Grasshoppers, katydids, and crickets are very common in the North Woods.

Appearance
Adults: Generally medium to large often stout-bodied insects. They possess four wings which they keep folded like a fan behind their backs when at rest. The first pair is leathery, i.e. somewhat thickened, while the second pair is thin, pleated and folded or rolled beneath front pair. Most species possess wings that are as long as the body or longer, although a few species have short wings and some lack wings altogether. Grasshoppers, katydids, and crickets possess chewing mouthparts and large back legs for jumping. This insect group possesses either short or long antennae. Females often have conspicuous ovipositors on the tips of their abdomens (which are often mistaken for stingers).

Nymphs: Immature nymphs are similar in form to adults but are smaller and lack fully developed wings or sexual structures, i.e. ovipositors (for females) or cerci (for males). Nymphs sometimes are a different color from the adults.

Habitats
Grasshoppers, katydids, and crickets are found in most types of terrestrial environments, essentially anywhere low growing plants are found such as prairies, fields, meadows, and areas adjacent to wooded sites. Many orthopteran species are found on the ground or a short distance above it on herbaceous plants or low growing shrubs. Other species are associated with trees.

Life Cycle
Grasshoppers, katydids, and crickets develop using paurometabolous metamorphosis, a type of simple metamorphosis. Adult females usually lay eggs at the end of summer or fall. Eggs hatch in spring and nymphs develop during spring and summer before maturing into adults. It usually takes one year to complete their life cycle.

Food

Many orthopterans are plant feeders. Some species are omnivorous, i.e. feeding on both plants and animal matter while others are scavengers on dead or decaying organic material. Some species are even predaceous on insects and other arthropods.

Sound Production

Many orthopterans are capable of producing sound. This is typically accomplished by rubbing specialized structures on two body parts together, a process called stridulation. There are different reasons for grasshoppers, katydids and crickets to make sound. Often males sing to attract females for mating. In other cases, they may signal distress when they are threatened or aggression when a male invades another's territory. Each orthopteran has a song specific to its species. The speed of these songs are dependent on the temperature; the number of beats per second will become slower or faster according to how cool or warm it is.

Don't confuse them with...

...true bugs. While some true bugs have somewhat large back legs and may resemble orthopterans, they have piercing-sucking mouthparts and wings that are folded flat and crosswise over their abdomen.

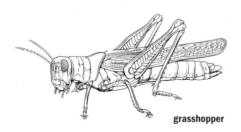

grasshopper

Grasshoppers
Family Acrididae

Appearance

Grasshoppers range in size from 1/2 to 3 inches long insects and are brownish, grayish, or greenish. They possess short, somewhat thicker antennae, considerably shorter than their body length. Their wings resemble grass blades which are held vertically along the length of the abdomen. They hear with a tympanum which is found on the first segment of the abdomen. Females possess short ovipositors.

Biology

Grasshoppers are active during the day. They are strictly plant feeders usually eating a variety of different species. A grasshopper lays it eggs in the soil by inserting its ovipositor and abdomen into the ground where it deposits a cluster of eggs. Grasshoppers are not as musical as other orthopterans. When they produce sound, they do so by rubbing peg-like structures on their back legs against their forewing producing a low buzzing song or by making a snapping sound with their wings as they fly (called crepitation).

Two-striped Grasshopper *Melanoplus bivittatus*

An easily identified *Melanoplus* grasshopper in a genus of difficult identifications. This spur-throated grasshopper is yellowish green over most of its body (but can be reddish brown) with olive green on top and two yellow stripes that start by its eyes and extends across the thorax back to its wings. The Two-striped Grasshopper prefers moist areas and is seldom on dry sites. Males possess wings about the length of their bodies and are good flyers but do not travel far while females have short wings and do not fly well. The Two-striped Grasshopper prefers broadleaf plants but will also feed on grasses. Can be a pest on corn crops.

Red-legged Grasshopper *Melanoplus femurrubrum*

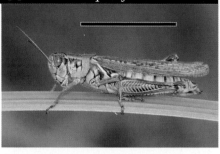

Though, by no means the only grasshopper with a red hind tibia, it is a very common and adaptable species found throughout North America except for northern Canada and Alaska. A type of spurthroated grasshopper that can be found in croplands, meadows and grasslands. Wings mottled and narrow, hind femur edged in red and hind tibia all red (often concealed when perched).

Carolina Locust *Dissosteira carolina*

Poorly named, for this species is neither a locust nor restricted to the Carolinas, but it is very common and distinctive. This is one of our larger grasshoppers, females growing as large as 2 ¼ inches. The Carolina Locust is a type of band-winged grasshopper and is known in Canada by the more appropriate name Black-winged Grasshopper. While its body is brown, reddish brown or gray, the hind wings are black with a yellow margin, which is easily seen when this grasshopper is flying. It is a good flier and is often found fluttering or hovering like a butterfly (see right photo). This grasshopper crepitates conspicuously while flying, i.e. it produces a popping sounds. It resembles "chick-a....chick-a....chick-a."

The hovering, fluttering courtship flight of the Carolina Locust is often seen during late summer.

Particularly common in sandy or gravelly open areas with little vegetation where it is well camouflaged. It is also common along roads, beaches, shorelines and unplanted fields. It feeds on many kinds of grasses and broadleaf plants.

Clear-winged Grasshopper *Camnula pellucida*

The Clear-winged Grasshopper is a type of band-winged grasshopper that does not have any bands on its wings! The hind wings are clear. Mottled forewings have a yellowish line that forms a V when it is not flying. Found in a variety of habitats, including undisturbed grassy meadows and roadsides where they feed mostly on grasses. They do not crepitate, i.e. make sound with their wings as they fly but they can stridulate with their wings.

Green-striped Grasshopper *Chortophaga viridifasciata*

This species is likely the first adult grasshopper encountered in spring, occurring in May and June but disappearing by early summer. This early-season appearance is enabled by the overwintering of a partially developed nymph (unlike most grasshoppers). It is a species of band-winged grasshopper that occurs in two color forms, either green (usually females) or brown (often males). While the abdomens are reddish brown in both color forms, they differ in having the head, thorax and outside surface of the back femur colored green or brown. Males are much smaller than females. Found especially in moist areas with grasses a foot tall or shorter. It prefers to eat grasses but will eat some forbs.

Crackling Locust *Trimerotropis verruculata verruculata*

Very wary and difficult to approach closely. And when they do fly they make very loud crepitations, hence the "crackling." The only dark *Trimerotropis* in the Great Lakes region. Usually on rocky ground.

Mottled Sand Grasshopper *Spharagemon collare*

Finely speckled black, white and yellow, this grasshopper nearly disappears on the sandy habitats it frequents. Very common on Great Lakes dunes but also found in dry woods and sandy roadsides. Note the well-defined ridge on top of the thorax cut by a single notch (the *Trimerotropis* species, which may also be found on sand, have a weakly defined ridge cut by two notches). Hind tibia solid orange. Wings pale yellow with broad black margin. Summer into fall.

Northern Marbled Grasshopper
Spharagemon marmorata marmorata

This beautiful subspecies is specialized for life on sandy pine barrens in the north; their marbled green coloration blends perfectly with ground-dwelling lichens and mosses. They eat blueberry leaves and likely other forbs. During long zigzag flights they crepitate loudly. Look for them in sandy and sparsely vegetated Jack Pine barrens especially in the U.P. of Michigan and northwest Wisconsin. Found from Minnesota east to New England and south to North Carolina. Mid July to mid September.

Northwestern Red-winged Grasshopper
Arphia pseudonietana

A late summer band-winged species of dry, open grasslands and upland fields. Hind wings usually reddish to pinkish with a broad black margin. Like other bandwinged grasshoppers, it can crepitate, i.e. make a snapping sound with its wings as it flies.

Family *Acrididae* GRASSHOPPERS

Sulphur-winged Grasshopper *Arphia sulphurea*

A mottled dark species of band-winged grasshopper with black-bordered yellow hind wings (visible only in flight). Common in fields, open woodlands, wood margins and along road-sides where it feeds on grasses. Unlike most other grasshoppers, it spends the winter as a nymph, maturing into an adult in May. Most common in June.

Coral-winged Grasshopper *Pardalophora apiculata*

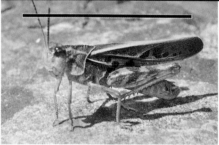

One of the first adult grasshoppers encountered during the North Woods summer, sometimes as early as May. Their bright pink-red ("coral") hind wings flash as they fly but they do not crepitate. This one was photographed in a burned area of a Jack Pine forest. They also like dry sandy fields. May to July.

Marsh Meadow Grasshopper *Chorthippus curtipennis*

One of the most common slant-faced grasshoppers in our area. Like its common name implies, it is found in meadows bordering marshes. Ideally the habitat is a mixture of grasses and flowers of medium to tall height. The male's soft stridulations are a common sound in marshes and meadows.

Graceful Sedge Grasshopper *Stethophyma gracile*

Truly a northern species that is only found in the northern U.S. and Canada. It feeds on sedges in wet areas such as wet shrub meadows, lake edges and sedge marshes. The male's loud rasping stridulations can be mistaken for that of a katydid. Yellowish green with few contrasting markings. July to September.

Family *Acrididae* GRASSHOPPERS

Pygmy Grasshoppers (Grouse Locusts) Family Tetrigidae

Appearance

The best way to recognize a pygmy grasshopper is by its pronotum which extends past the abdomen, covering the wings and then tapering at the tip. Beware of identifying pygmy grasshoppers by color alone; coloration is highly variable—even between individuals of the same species. They are relatively small, measuring between 1/2 to 3/4 inch long. They have short antennae.

Biology

This is one of the few group of grasshoppers that overwinters as adults. You can see pygmy grasshoppers during spring and early summer. Found along the shores of ponds and streams where there is wet soil.

Pygmy Grasshopper *Tetrix arenosa*

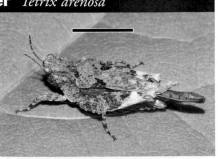

Found at marsh or pond edges. Overwinters as an adult and reproduces in late spring (underwater?). No hard and fast rule can be given for the color of this species. It is HIGHLY variable, ranging from pale, nearly white, on the back to extremely dark, nearly black. *Tetrix* species identified based on minute differences in the shape of the front of the head.

Black-sided Grouse Locust *Tettigidea lateralis*

An attractive little species of open woodlands that is found from Manitoba east to the Canadian maritime province, Nova Scotia. One of four *Tettigidea* species in North America. Overwinters as an adult and reproduces in late spring. White of the face continues onto thorax and is distinctive to this species. Many antennal segments (over 14). Some entomologists place the *Tettigidea* in a separate family—the Batrachideidae.

Katydids
Family Tettigoniidae

Appearance

Katydids are usually green insects possessing very long, hair-like, antennae that are at least as long as their bodies and often longer. Wings are long and may be narrow or broad and leaf-like and are held tent-like over their bodies. The left hand wing usually lays over the right side wing. Katydids have long, stilt-like hind legs and possess a tympanum, i.e. an ear, in the tibia of their front legs (see photo right). Katydids also have flattened sword-like or blade-like ovipositors.

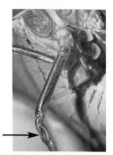

Note the tympanum on the foreleg; it is the organ which enables katydids to hear.

Biology

Look for katydids in shrubs and trees. Many are plant feeders, although some are omnivorous and a few prey on insects and other invertebrates. Most katydids insert their eggs into leaves or twigs. Katydids are prodigious song makers. Males make sound by rubbing structures on their forewings together which produce a generally raspy song. Listen for them at night when they are active.

Look for katydids along brushy roadsides or along trails in late summer. Key in on their songs.

Broadwinged Bush Katydid *Scudderia pistillata*

This katydid is a type of bush katydid (sometimes called "false katydid"). It has broad leaf-like, nearly parallel-sided forewings. Folded hindwings extend beyond the end of the abdomen and are longer than the forewings. The Broadwinged Bush Katydid is light green and is typically found in shrubs in damp areas.

Males produce songs at dusk consisting of five to eight rapid pulses, getting louder by the end of the song. Watch for adults starting in July.

Sword-bearing Conehead *Neoconocephalus ensiger*

With a name befitting an alien from outer space, the Sword-bearing Conehead is merely a humble katydid found in wet fields and meadows. It has long slender wings and antennae that are inserted behind a small knob on the top of its head. Large, measuring as long as 2 ½ inches including the wings. Females possess a particularly conspicuous ovipositor, as long as one inch. The distinctive song consists of a series of sharp, hissing pulses, about ten per second, heard both at night and day. It is an adult from July through September.

Slender Meadow Katydid *Conocephalus fasciatus fasciatus*

This slender katydid is green with some brown on its head, thorax, and wings. The wings are little longer than the body with the hind wings just exceeding the length of the forewings. The apex of the head does not extend beyond the base of the antennae. The Slender Meadow Katydid is relatively small growing to one inch in length, including the wings. It is found in grassy, weedy areas in meadows, pine woods and roadsides; in dry areas as well as near wet sites. It feeds mostly on grasses. The song is somewhat weak and is composed of a trilling or buzzing sound that lasts for about ten to thirty seconds followed by a distinct "tick, tick, tick" sound. Their singing can be heard during the day as well as at night. The Slender Meadow Katydid is first active in late July.

Gladiator Meadow Katydid *Orchelium gladiator*

This species shows some brown on the wings. The wings are similar in length and extend beyond the abdomen. Gladiator Meadow Katydids are common in damp areas, especially tall grass meadows. The song is a series of buzzes alternating with ticks. Adults are present from mid July through September.

Crickets
Family Gryllidae

Appearance

Crickets possess very long, hair-like antennae that are at least as long as their bodies. Their wings are held flat over their abdomens. Crickets have three tarsal segments in their legs and have needle-like ovipositors. Like katydids, crickets possess a tympanum on each of their front legs.

Biology

Common in fields, roadside ditches and other open areas where they are found on the ground or on low vegetation. Tree crickets be found in trees and shrubs. They are often omnivorous, feeding on both animal and plant matter, while some are strictly plant feeders and a few are just predaceous. Crickets lay their eggs in the soil or in plants. Many crickets are quite musical producing songs, like katydids, by rubbing their front wings together. Unlike katydids, the right hand wing of a cricket lays over the left one.

Fall Field Cricket *Gryllus pennsylvanicus*

Our common summer/fall cricket. Male's wings nearly cover the abdomen while female's only cover 3/5th of the body. Large, conspicuous spines on back legs. Females have a spear-like ovipositor that is as long as its body. Found in grassy meadows and prairies where it eats both animal and plant matter. First mature in late July (Spring Field Cricket only seen in spring). Song is a slow methodical series of chirps.

Blackhorned Tree Cricket *Oecanthus nigricornus*

Pale green with black on its head, thorax, antennae and the ends of its legs. Wings just cover the abdomen. Males have widened, teardrop shaped wings; female's more slender. Common in fields on weeds, shrubs and small trees. Feeds on insects, like aphids, as well as plants. Song is a loud continuous trilling. Late July through September.

Camel Crickets
Family Rhaphidophoridae

Appearance

Sometimes called cave crickets, camel crickets are brownish, hump-backed insects that range from $1/3$ to $1^1/3$ inches in length. They possess very long, hair-like antennae, about twice the length of their bodies. They have conspicuously spiny tibiae. Camel crickets lack wings and females have an elongate ovipositor.

Biology

Camel crickets are active at night and are typically found in dark, moist places, such as under logs and stones, in animal burrows, in hollow trees and tree holes, and caves and spaces under structures without foundations. Camel crickets feed primarily on weakened or dead insects or other invertebrates although they occasionally feed on plant material. Unlike other orthopterans, they lack any stridulating organs to produce sound.

Spotted Camel Cricket · *Ceuthophilus maculatus*

This is a common camel cricket species in the North Woods. This medium-sized camel cricket grows as long as a $1/2$ inch. The body is mostly brown with black and light patches on the dorsal surface of the thorax. It is common under stones, logs and leaf litter, particularly in drier wooded areas. They are also commonly found indoors, particularly in basements.

Walkingsticks
Order Phasmida

Diversity
There are four families and 41 species in the United States. Only one or two species of the common walkingsticks (family Heteronemiidae) are found in the North Woods where they can be common.

Appearance
Adults: Walkingsticks are large twig-like insects with very long, slender brownish or greenish bodies. They have long antennae and chewing mouthparts that point forward. These slow moving insects lack wings. Males are usually smaller and more slender compared to females.

Nymphs: The immature nymphs are very similar to adults only smaller.

Habitats
They are found in wooded areas, associated with hardwood trees and shrubs. They are normally not found in urban landscapes.

Life Cycle
Walkingsticks develop using paurometabolous metamorphosis, a type of simple metamorphosis. Adult females typically drop their eggs from trees, letting them fall down to the forest floor. When nymphs hatch, they climb up shrubs and small trees to feed. Once they mature into adults, they typically move into larger trees.

Food
Both adults and nymphs feed on the leaves of a variety of hardwood trees and shrubs. Sometimes their feeding can severely defoliate plants.

Protection From Enemies
Walkingsticks protect themselves by using mimicry. They are hard to see, especially when they hold still, because of their resemblance to sticks and twigs. They will also sway to mimic a twig in the wind. This helps protect them from natural enemies, like birds. Interestingly, walkingsticks are one of the few insects that can regenerate lost legs, although this ability is restricted to immature nymphs.

Don't confuse them with...
...stilt bugs. Stilt bugs are slender and twig-like but have piercing-sucking mouthparts. They are also much smaller than walkingsticks. Otherwise walkingsticks are distinctive and you are unlikely to confuse them with other insects.

Northern Walkingstick   *Diapheromera femorata*

Walkingsticks in the North Woods? Most of us associate walkingsticks with tropical, or at least southern, climes. But the Northern Walkingstick is a common and widespread species in the southern regions of the North Woods. Adults are 2 ¹/₂ to 3 inches long and vary in color from brown to green to mottled colors in between. This walkingstick feeds on a variety of hardwood trees and shrubs, especially oaks, cherry and basswood. Northern Walkingsticks mature into adults by August and then mate during late summer or fall. Females randomly drop eggs to the ground during fall until frost. Nymphs hatch during late spring. Although a few eggs hatch the following spring, most remain dormant for a year and hatch during the second spring. Northern walkingsticks can occur in local areas in large numbers and severely defoliate stands of trees.

♀

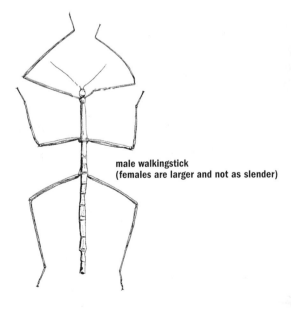

**male walkingstick
(females are larger and not as slender)**

Earwigs
Order Dermaptera

Diversity
There are six families and 22 species in the United States. Earwigs are uncommon in the North Woods.

Appearance
Adults: Earwigs are medium sized, brownish to blackish beetle-like insects with somewhat flattened bodies. They have medium length antennae and chewing mouthparts. Their first pair of wings are typically leathery and very short with a pair of rounded membranous wings hidden underneath.

They are distinctive because they possess a pair of strong pinchers (cerci) on the tip of their abdomen. You can distinguish between the sexes as males have stout, strongly curved cerci that are widely separated at the base while females possess slender, straight pinchers that are close together. Earwigs use these cerci to protect themselves and to grab and hold prey. You can also distinguish between males and females as males possess ten abdominal segments while female only have eight.

Nymphs: Nymphs are similar to adults except they are smaller. They will also lack wing pads when they first hatch. All immature earwigs have female-like, slender straight cerci. Young earwigs are generally lighter in color than adults.

Habitats
Earwigs are nocturnal and hide during the day in cracks and crevices as well as under objects and debris, such as leaves, mulch, stones, bark, and logs. Earwigs are also commonly found on plants, especially flower blossoms.

Life Cycle
Earwigs develop using paurometabolous metamorphosis, a type of simple metamorphosis. Eggs are typically laid in small constructed nests in the soil. Female earwigs are very maternal, an unusual trait for insects. They guard and protect their eggs and newly hatched young.

Food
Earwigs are generally scavengers feeding on damaged and decaying plant matter as well as weakened or dead insects and other small organisms. Some earwigs also feed on healthy plant material.

Protecting Themselves

There is an old story that claims that earwigs climb into people's ear while they are sleeping. This of course is untrue! However, they will try to pinch with their cerci. Fortunately most earwigs are not capable of inflicting anything painful. Some earwigs can also secrete a foul-smelling liquid from their abdomen to ward off enemies.

Don't confuse them with...

...beetles with short wings, especially rove beetles. These odd true beetles could be confused with earwigs. However, beetles lack strong pinchers on the abdomen.

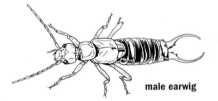

male earwig

earwig attempting to pinch with cerci

European Earwig *Forficula auricularia*

Originally from Europe, this species was introduced into the U.S. in the early 1900s and is now common throughout much of the country. The European Earwig is reddish brown with yellow legs. They are found in cool, damp conditions in all types of cracks and crevices as well as on flowers and other herbaceous plants. European Earwigs can be quite common in gardens. They spend the winter as mated pairs. The female lays eggs during early spring after which time the male is forced out of the nest. She protects the eggs and then cares for the nymphs for several weeks after they hatch before they are on their own.

Cockroaches
Order Blattaria

Diversity

There are four families and 50 species in the United States. Two species of cockroaches are somewhat common outdoors in the North Woods. Several different species can be very common indoors.

Appearance

Adults: Small to large sized insects with a flattened, oval shaped body, long antennae (one-half the length of the body or longer) and chewing mouthparts. When looking at a cockroach from above, its head is hidden from view by a plate-like structure called the pronotum. The strong legs are covered with spines. Cockroaches found outdoors in the North Woods possess four wings that are longer than the abdomen. The first pair is leathery while the second pair is more membranous. Female wood cockroaches have short wings, exposing part of the abdomen.

Nymphs: Nymphs are very similar in form to adults but are smaller and lack fully developed wings.

Habitats

Cockroaches that live outdoors in the North Woods are typically found in wooded sites or adjacent areas. They are usually found in rotting logs or under loose bark.

Life Cycle

Cockroaches develop using paurometabolous metamorphosis, a type of simple metamorphosis. Eggs are produced inside a case, called an ootheca where generally between 30 to 50 eggs are found. These oothecae are often deposited soon after they are formed into safe, protected sites where they wait until the eggs hatch. Some species hang on to the oothecae until just before they eggs are ready to hatch while in other species the eggs hatch while the oothecae are held internally in the females and the nymphs are born live (viviparous).

Food

Cockroaches that live outdoors in the North Woods feed primarily on various types of decaying organic matter. Cockroaches found indoors feed broadly on essentially all types of human food products.

Don't confuse them with...

...beetles, true bugs or earwigs. The first pair of wings of beetles are hardened and their antennae are generally not long (except in the long-horn beetles). True bugs have hemelytrous wings, i.e. part leathery and part membranous as well piercing-sucking mouthparts. Earwigs have short wings, medium length antennae and possess pincher-like cerci on the tip of their abdomens.

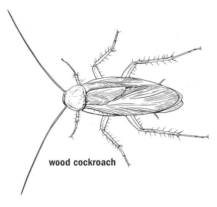

wood cockroach

Wood Cockroach *Parcoblatta species*

This is NOT the cockroach of homes and buildings. This wood cockroach lives in wooded areas in rotting logs and under loose bark. It does not survive indoors and is not a pest. The adult male is dark brown, with light colored bands on the edge of the body near the head. It also has long, well developed wings and can fly, although it can't stay in the air for long. The female is smaller with very short wings and cannot fly. This cockroach is attracted to light and can be common around yard lights or car lights. Females lay eggs in stumps, under loose bark and in piles of firewood. The eggs hatch during summer and the immature nymphs spend the winter in protected sites. The nymphs continue developing the following spring eventually maturing into adults.

True Bugs, Cicadas, Aphids, etc. Order Hemiptera

Diversity
There are 90 families and 11,298 species in North America. True bugs are very common in the North Woods.

Appearance
Adults: Form, size and color are quite variable and diverse. They possess piercing-sucking mouthparts which can be very short and beak-like or long and slender. They have short to moderate length slender antennae. They usually possess four wings. The first pair of wings can be hemelytrous, i.e. partly leathery and part membranous (the true bugs) or uniformly thickened or membranous, (cicadas, hoppers, aphids and others). The second pair of wings is membranous. Some species lack wings (Some populations and even some individual adults can have the wings reduced or absent.). Many hemipterans have sawlike or piercing ovipositors for laying eggs in plant tissue or bark.

Nymphs: Similar in form to adults except they are smaller and lack wings. Wings pads are present in older nymphs. It is common for the nymphs to be different colors from adults. True bugs use simple metamorphosis to develop.

Habitats
Most hemipterans are terrestrial, inhabiting a wide variety of different habitats. They are often found associated with plants. Some are aquatic living in or on the surface of water or are semiaquatic living on shores.

Life Cycle
The hemipterans develop using paurometabolous metamorphosis, a type of simple metamorphosis. The life cycle varies with the particular insect. Some have complex life cycles requiring multiple plant hosts. Some hemipterans overwinter as adults and lay eggs in the spring while others overwinter as eggs.

Food
Most are plant feeders, although a few are predacious, a few omnivorous, and a few are even parasitic on the blood of animals or birds.

Don't confuse them with...

...beetles. The first pair of wings of beetles are modified into a hard shell known as elytra. Beetles also have mandibles and chewing mouthparts. Some hemipterans can be confused with grasshoppers, crickets, or katydids. However, they have chewing mouthparts and large back legs. Hemipterans either fold their wings roof-like over their abdomens or cross them flat on their backs.

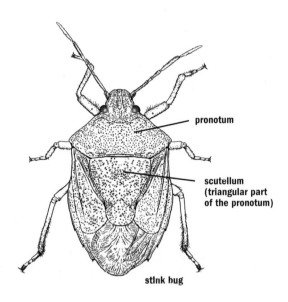

pronotum

scutellum
(triangular part
of the pronotum)

stink bug

Water Scorpions
Family Nepidae

Appearance

Most are slender brownish walkingstick-like insects ranging up to 1½ inches long with an elongate prothorax. There is one uncommon species is a smaller, oval, medium-bodied insect. All water scorpions have modified front legs, called raptorial legs, that allow them to capture and hold their prey. They possess a pair of long breathing tubes, as long as their body, protruding from the tips of their abdomen. Water scorpions have very short antennae which are rarely noticed.

Biology

Water scorpions are aquatic, living in ponds and along the shores of lakes, amongst aquatic weeds. They obtain oxygen at the water surface using a pair of long breathing tubes. Water scorpions can store air under their wings if they wish to swim under the surface. They are not good swimmers and spend much of their time clinging to submerged plants. They swim by rowing with their middle and back legs, stroking them alternatively, although if they wish to swim more quickly, they use these legs in unison. They are predacious, feeding on insects and other aquatic invertebrate animals. If threatened, water scorpions will play dead. Water scorpions overwinter as adults and typically insert eggs into aquatic plants in the spring. Adults are active throughout spring and most of the summer.

Brown Water Scorpion *Ranatra fusca*

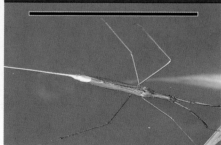

The only thing "scorpion" about this insect may be its long breathing tube coming out of the end of the abdomen. The Brown Water Scorpion is up to 1 ¾ inches long, not including its breathing tube, which is nearly one inch by itself. Unlike most other water scorpions, this species lays eggs in mud banks that lack plants.

Giant Water Bugs
Family Belostomatidae

Appearance

These large, one to two inch, brown insects are broadly oval and some-what flattened. Their front legs are raptorial, i.e. they are modified for grabbing prey. Their hind legs are broad and oar-like. Giant water bugs have short, inconspicuous breathing tubes. They possess very, short inconspicuous antennae.

Biology

These insects are common in ponds and lakes. They breathe using a pair of small retractable flap-like organs on the tip of their abdomen. Like water scorpions, giant water bugs swim with their middle and hind legs, using them alternately but will use them together when swimming more quickly. They are predators, feeding on other insects as well as tadpoles, snails and even small fish. Eggs are generally laid on stones, logs, plants and other inanimate objects. In some giant water bug species, they lay their eggs on the back of the males which is where they remain until they hatch. It is common for giant water bugs to leave the water and fly around. They are attracted to lights and it is common to find them around ball fields, parking lots, tennis courts and other well lit areas. Because of this, they are sometimes called "electric light bugs." Giant water bugs can bite if handled carelessly. They overwinter as adults and lay eggs in the spring. They have one generation a year and adults are seen during spring and most of the summer.

Giant Water Bug *Lethocerus americanus*

Many folks first see this giant of an insect on warm summer evenings near their own homes; They occasionally leave the water in search of mates or another home and are attracted to lights. It is common to find giant water bugs in yards, parking lots, ball fields and other places where they are attracted to outdoor lighting. They are olive brown and may reach 2 3/8 inches long. The Giant Water Bug is common in ponds, swimming on the bottom amongst vegetation where it feeds on insects, tadpoles, small fish, snails and even salamanders! This insect is some-times referred to as "toe biter" because of its ability to painfully bite people if mishandled. Adults overwinter in shallow, muckish areas of ponds and lakes.

Water Boatmen
Family Corixidae

Appearance

A soft-bodied, elongate, oval and somewhat flattened insect, a water boatman is no larger than ½ inch long. Water boatmen are generally dark brown with dark crosslines. It possesses short scoop-like front legs and long paddle-like back legs. The wings are uniformly textured.

Biology

Commonly found in freshwater ponds and lakes and less commonly in slow moving streams and small stagnant bodies of water. They breathe at the water surface through the thorax but can also carry a bubble of air under its wings and around its abdomen. Water boatmen can occur in large numbers and are very agile swimmers, typically moving very erratically on the water's surface. The swim moving their back legs synchronously. Most water boatmen feed on algae, diatoms, nematodes and other tiny aquatic animals. Some are predacious on small insects, especially midge and mosquito larvae. Water boatmen overwinter as adults and are active spring and most of the summer.

Water Boatman *Sigara species*

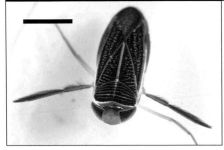

A streamlined bug made for the water; Scoop-like front legs and long paddle-like back legs move in synchrony as they literally row through the water. They can be quite numerous in freshwater ponds and lakes. Spring through summer.

Backswimmers
Family Notonectidae

Appearance

Oval, elongate insects with a convex dorsum (top surface). The first pair of legs are normal sized while the last pair of legs are long, broad and oar-like. The antennae are very short and inconspicuous. Most backswimmers are about 3/5 inch long. They are generally light colored on their dorsal surface, lacking dark crosslines and dark underneath. This camouflages them from fish that swim below.

Biology

Backswimmers spend much of their time near the surface of ponds, swimming mostly on their backs. They breathe at the surface of the water through the tip of their abdomen. Backswimmers can carry a store of oxygen on the underside of their abdomen as well as under their wings. Their pattern of movement is less erratic than water boatmen. They commonly rest with their body at a 45 degree angle with their head down and their hind legs stretched out. They are ready to swim away quickly if necessary. Like water boatmen, backswimmers "row" with their back legs moving in tandem. They are predacious, feeding on small aquatic invertebrate animals and even occasionally on tadpoles and small fish and can bite people if handled carelessly. Backswimmers lay their eggs on or into submerged plant tissue as well as on rocks. Backswimmers overwinter as adults and lay eggs in the spring. Watch for them from spring through summer.

Backswimmer *Notonecta species*

Backswimmers do indeed do the back stroke; Hind legs move in unison as they row through the water. But their movements are less herky-jerky than the water boatman. Spring through summer.

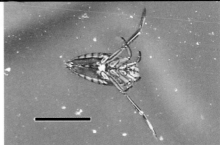

Water Striders
Family Gerridae

Appearance

Slender bodied insects ranging in size from ¼ to over ½ inch long. The second and third of pairs of legs are long and slender while the first pair is short. Water striders possess slender, moderate length antennae. They typically have black or brown bodies with many of them lacking wings.

In shallow clear waters, the water strider creates a unique shadow of its body and the depression in the water's surface its legs create.

Biology

Water striders are common on the surface of ponds and slow moving steams, sometimes occurring in large numbers. The tarsi are covered with very fine hairs which allows a water strider to skate over the surface of the water. It is difficult for those hairs get wet, but if they do a water strider will

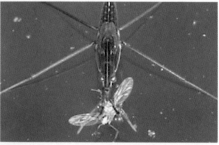

This water strider has captured an insect.

sink. Only the middle and hind pair of legs touch the water. The first set of legs are held in front of them and above the water. Adults spend the winter in protected sites, e.g under rocks or leaves on land near the water.

Common Water Strider *Aquarius remigis*

Ubiquitous on sluggish waters, the Common Water Strider does just that—it strides over the surface of the water. It's really more like lunging than striding. It has a silvery pubescence on the underside of its body. Look for Common Water striders during spring and most the summer. Formerly called *Gerris remigis*.

Shore Bugs
Family Saldidae

Appearance

Small, usually between ⅛ to ¼ inch long, oval, flattened insects. Shore bugs are dark-colored insects, typically brown or black and white markings. They have moderate length antennae and large eyes. Shore bugs are distinctive because they possess four to five closed cells in the membrane of the wing.

Biology

Shore bugs are found on the shores of streams, rivers, ponds and lakes. They can run quickly and like to hide under plant debris, small stones and other objects. They can also jump and sustain short bursts of flight. Shore bugs are usually predacious on other small insects and other invertebrates, although they may occasionally scavenge on dead specimens. They overwinter as adults and lay eggs in the spring. You can find adults during spring and most of the summer.

Shore Bug *Pentacora ligata*

Firm sand on Great Lake's beaches is a great place to look for this attractive shore bug. Also found on rocky shores along streams and rivers; especially the exposed rocks actually in the river. It is blackish with yellow spots. It is distinctive from other shore bugs because it has five close cells in the membranous part of its hemelytra.

Shore Bug *Salda or Saldula species*

Open sandy shoreline is where this shore bug was photographed. Note the bulging red eyes and all black body. Like many shore bugs, this one was fast and wary; scurrying across the sand at the first hint of trouble.

Lace Bugs
Family Tingidae

Appearance

These are small insects, measuring about ⅛ to ¼ inch long. The head is concealed under an expanded hood-like pronotum. Their pronotum and wings are sculptured giving them a lacy appearance. They are often brownish or grayish, often mottled with black spots.

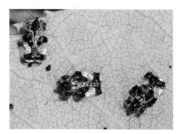

Biology

Lace bugs are slow-moving insects, feeding gregariously on the underside of deciduous tree and shrub leaves, especially oak, hackberry, willow, chokecherry and hawthorn and other plants in the rose family. This feeding

Rarely will you find a single lace bug; they are gregarious and feed in groups on the undersides of leaves.

causes a speckled discoloration on the upper surface of leaves. Lace bugs overwinter as adults and lay eggs on leaves in the spring.

Hawthorn Lace Bug *Corythucha cydoniae*

Look on the UNDERSIDES of tree leaves for these bizarre insects. Visible veins on flat transparent wings give it a lacy look. And they are often found in groups with nymphs. Adult is whitish gray with two black bars across its wings. Leaves of hawthorn, juneberry, crab apple, chokeberry and other trees and shrubs in the rose family are its primary food. Though this specimen was identified to species, many *Corythucha* lace bugs look similar. Hawthorn Lace Bugs are active spring and summer.

Plant Bugs
Family Miridae

Appearance

Small to medium sized insects, $1/6$ to $3/8$ inch long, with moderate length antennae and usually an oval or elongate body, although the shape is variable. Many are green or brown and blend in with their surroundings but some can be brightly colored, e.g. red or yellow. Plant bugs possess a cuneus, a triangular segment of the thickened portion of the wings and one or two closed cells in the membranous part of the wings. This membranous section of the wings is characteristically bent down. A few plant bugs lack wings or have shortened wing.

Biology

This is the most common group of true bugs. They are typically found on plants where most species are herbivores. Some are scavengers and a few are predacious on other insects. Plant bugs spend the winter as eggs, typically laid into plant tissue.

Alfalfa Plant Bug *Adelphocoris lineaolatus*

Another alien from Europe that has gained pest status; The Alfalfa Plant Bug made its North American appearance in the mid 20th century and has become a problem in seed alfalfa fields. It is also found on wildflowers in summer.

Meadow Plant Bug *Stenotus binotatus*

Originally a European species, they were accidentally introduced into North America a century ago. Like the Latin specific epithet *binotatus* suggests, it has two bold spots on the prothorax. The similar Alfalfa Plant Bug lacks these. Commonly found in meadows, fields and ditches on a variety of grasses during July and August.

Tarnished Plant Bug *Lygus lineolaris*

"Tarnished" probably refers to this abundant insect's brown with yellow, white and black markings, but it could also refer to its damage to plants it feeds on. Color is variable as demonstrated in these two photos. But no matter what base color the specimen is, it will always show a yellowish heart-shaped marking on the anterior of its wings (sometimes looks more like a Y). Unlike most other plant bugs, Tarnished Plant Bugs feed on a wide variety of herbaceous plants as well as some trees and shrubs. Tarnished plant bugs are active spring, summer and into fall.

Fourlined Plant Bug *Poecilocapsus lineatus*

Gardens are where you may encounter Fourlined Plant Bugs as they feed on many types of perennials as well as on fruits such as gooseberry; Also feed occasionally on trees and shrubs including dogwood, viburnum and sumac. They are greenish yellow with four black stripes down the wings. Fourlined plant bugs overwinter as eggs laid in clusters into slits near the tops of canes of currants, brambles and other woody plants. Eggs hatch in May. Fourlined Plant Bugs are active into early July.

Plant bug *Metriorrhynchomiris dislocatus*

This striking red and black plant bug is most often seen along woodland trails; In some areas mostly found on species of *Iris*, *Lychnis* or *Geranium*. But don't be fooled by this photo—Several color variations can occur: all black, red pronotum with black wings, orange and black, etc.

Plant Bug *Collaria meilleurii*

You may get your feet wet trying to find this plant bug; It prefers wet sedge meadows. But it can also be found in dryer fields of grasses (*Poa* species).

Plant Bug *Capsus ater*

Roadside grasses are the microhabitat of *Capsus ater*. Like the Alfalfa Plant Bug above, it is an introduced species from Europe. The all black form seen here is most common but individuals with a red pronotum are also encountered. The second antennal segment is swollen near the end. May to July.

Damsel Bugs
Family Nabidae

Appearance

Medium-sized slender insects, between $3/16$ to $1/2$ inch long. They are typically dull brownish or grayish while a few are shiny black. They have a somewhat enlarged femur on their front leg as well as many small closed cells around the edge of the membrane of the hemelytra. Some species possess very short wings.

Biology

Look for damsel bugs on plants where they feed on other small insects and arthropods, such as aphids, scale crawlers, leafhoppers, spider mites, insect eggs and small larvae, including caterpillars and beetles. Damsel bugs overwinter as adults and can have several generations in a year. Some species are attracted to lights.

Common Damsel Bug *Nabis americoferus*

The Common Damsel Bug is a common predator of insects in old fields and meadows. It is yellowish brown with a faint dark mark on its head and pronotum. It is found on herbaceous plants and shrubs. Look for Common Damsel Bugs during spring and summer. It spends the winter as an adult under dead leaves.

Black Damsel Bug *Nabicula subcoleoptrata*

Shiny black body, exposed abdomen and short wings (rare individuals may have wings that cover the abdomen) are clues to identifying the Black Damsel Bug. Pale yellow around the edge of the abdomen. This is a known predator of Meadow Plant Bugs (*Stenotus binotatus*) (see page 53) but also feeds on a wide variety of insects including aphids and small caterpillars. Found mainly during early summer.

Minute Pirate Bugs
Family Anthocoridae

Appearance
Very small, between 1/14 to 1/5 inch long flattened insects. Minute pirate bugs are typically shiny black with whitish wings and somewhat diamond-shaped.

Biology
Minute pirate bugs usually occur on flowers and occasionally on trees where they are predacious on small insects, insect eggs and mites. These small insects can bite people if they land on them, administering a surprisingly painful bite. Fortunately this is just accidental and they do not leave lasting injuries. Swarms of migrating minute pirate bugs can be encountered during September and early October. They are strongly attracted to blue. Minute pirate bugs overwinter as adults.

Insidious Flower Bug *Orius insidiosus*

An Insidiosus Flower Bug is only "insidious" to the thrips, aphids, spider mites and insect eggs that it feeds on. It has a black head, thorax and base of the wings. The rest of the wings has a yellowish band followed by a pair of black triangles with the membranous part of the wings whitish. It overwinters as an adult under fallen leaves. Active spring and summer.

Assassin Bugs & Ambush Bugs Family Reduviidae

Appearance

Slender to stout-bodied insects, usually medium sized. They possess a short beak which fits into a groove on the underside of the head. The abdomen of many species widen in the middle often extending beyond the wings. They are generally colored green or brown although some can be brightly colored. Some of these insects have raptorial front legs.

Note the beak tucked under the head on this Spined Assassin Bug.

Biology

Assassin bugs and ambush bugs are predacious, feeding on other insects. They are typically found on plants as well as in leaf litter, under stones and debris. Ambush bugs are commonly found on flowers where they use camouflage to hide and feed on insects that land there, some twice their size. They paralyze prey by toxins in their saliva which acts in seconds.

A mating pair of Jagged Ambush Bugs; females are mostly yellow.

Male Jagged Ambush Bugs are much darker than females.

Spined Assassin Bug *Sinea diadema*

The Spined Assassin commonly hunts for prey along the vertical surfaces of stems where it likes to wait motionless, head down, and ambush unwary insects traveling up the stems. It is colored to blend in—brown or reddish brown. It is a somewhat stout insect with a pear-shaped abdomen. The Spined Assassin Bug is commonly found on herbaceous plants in fields and meadows. It It is common spring and summer.

Assassin Bug *Zelus exsanguis*

Assassins must have the right tools to kill, and *Zelus* does; Sticky hairs on the front legs help capture and hold prey. Light green body color helps it blend in with the grasses, herbaceous plants, shrubs and low trees where it hunts. It is common spring and summer in wooded sites and edges.

Jagged Ambush Bug *Phymata pennsylvanica*

A crazy looking insect with raptorial front legs designed for capturing insects. It is sexually dimorphic; The male is greenish or yellowish with black markings. Female is yellow-green. It typically hides on matching colored flowers and "ambushes" unsuspecting insects. Despite its small size, an ambush bug will capture bees, butterflies and other insects much larger than itself. The Jagged Ambush Bug overwinters as an adult and lays eggs in the spring. Adults mature during summer.

Stilt Bugs
Family Berytidae

Appearance
Slender, slow moving, insects with long thread-like antennae and legs.
Winter as adults and lay eggs in the spring. Adults mature by summer.

Biology
Typically found on plants. Most feed on plant sap, although a few are
predacious on insects.

Spined Stilt Bug *Jalysus wickhami*

Look for the long legs, clubbed
antennae and long "swollen"
abdomen of these interesting
creatures. Reddish brown with
punctures on prothorax.
Common on plants in fields and
gardens, including plants in the
evening primrose and nightshade
families. It is also predacious,
feeding on aphids and on horn-
worm eggs.

Seed Bugs
Family Lygaeidae

Appearance
Most are orange and black while a few are brownish. Five conspicuous
veins in the wings. Abdominal spiracles found on top of the body.

Biology
Found especially on milkweeds where they feed on seeds. Bright colors
warn predators that they taste bad. Winter as adults.

Small Milkweed Bug *Lygaeus kalmii*

Milkweed is the key to finding
this species. It is found from
spring through summer in
fields and meadows where it
feeds on the seeds of milkweed.
Orange markings on its black
wings, somewhat form an X.
Also it has an orange mark on
its head and an orange band
across it thorax. (inset: nymph)

Leaf-footed Bugs
Family Coreidae

Appearance

Moderate to large stout-bodied insects, leaf-footed bugs are typically dark colored. They have moderate length antennae with a head narrower than the pronotum. They possess well developed scent glands on their thorax which allows them to give off a distinctive odor to deter predators. The membrane of their wings possesses many veins. Some species have a leaf-like expansion on their hind legs.

Biology

Leaf-footed bugs are plant-feeders, usually on the seed-bearing frit or on the exposed seeds or cones. Some species are general feeders while others feed on a particular group of plants. Leaf-footed bugs overwinter as adults, often in plant debris. Leaf-footed bugs are active during spring and summer.

Squash Bug *Anasa tristis*

Though a leaf-footed bug in the Family Coreidae, the Squash Bug actually lacks the flattened hind leg section that the other members of the family have. It is sometimes quite common in gardens and can be a pest of squash and pumpkins. Note that this specimen is laying golden eggs on a leaf.

Western Conifer Seed Bug *Leptoglossus occidentalis*

This bug did not arrive in the eastern U.S. until the 1980s. The Western Conifer Seed Bug is reddish brown with a white zigzag line across the center of its wings. The long, conspicuous back legs possess the family namesake—leaflike enlargements. It has orange and black stripes on its abdomen. They are found on pine, feeding on the green cones and needles. Overwinters as an adult. It is common for this insect to take shelter in homes.

Broad-headed Bugs
Family Alydidae

Appearance

Medium sized insects with a long, narrow brownish or blackish body and medium length antennae. They have a large head that is as wide or wider than the thorax and nearly as long. The membrane of the wings has numerous veins. Broad-headed bugs have well developed scent glands on the thorax which gives off a foul odor.

Biology

Broad-headed bugs are plant feeders and are found on herbaceous plants, grasses and weeds in woodlands, grassy fields and roadsides. Some broad-head bugs mimic ants. They also use odors to protect themselves from would be predators. Adults are active during summer.

Some nymphs are amazing ant mimics (*Alydus*).

Broad-headed Bug *Alydus eurinus*

The nymphs do an amazing job of mimicking an ant (see photo above). The adult is brown with uniformly colored antennae and light colored markings along the edge of the abdomen. It is commonly found on bush clover and is common from June to September.

Broad-headed Bug *Megalotoma quinquespinosus*

Lovely reds, oranges and browns are the warm colors of this broad-headed bug. There is whitish band on the antennae about 2/3 out from the head. It is found along the edge of wooded areas and adjacent fields where it feeds on a variety of herbaceous plants including Veiny Pea (*Lathyrus venosus*).

Broad-headed Bug *Protenor belfragei*

Not really broad-headed at all, still *Protenor belfragei* is included in the Family Alydidae. Often found in wetter grassy areas such as marshes and sedge meadows, but also damp road edges. Adults from July until first frost.

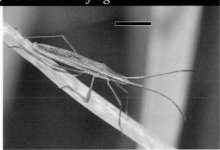

Scentless Plant Bugs Family Rhopalidae

Appearance
Small to medium, moderately oval insects. They are generally brownish or light colored insects, although some species are brightly colored. They have an average sized head with medium length antennae. Scentless plant bugs have many veins in the membrane of their wings. They lack scent glands.

Biology
Scentless? The name is from the lack of a large scent gland opening by the hind legs that most bugs have. They are plant feeders and are primarily found on weeds and other herbaceous plants. A few feed on trees. Look for scentless plant bugs during mid to late summer.

Boxelder Bug *Boisea trivittata*

Boxelder bugs feed on herbaceous plants and seeds they find on the ground during spring and early summer. But then in mid-summer, they become true to their common name and move to female seed-bearing Boxelder trees where they lay eggs on trunks, branches and leaves. They can be a nuisance when they enter homes in large numbers.

Stink Bugs
Family Pentatomidae

Appearance

Moderate to large insects that are ovoid or triangular in shape. Typically green or brown (some brightly colored or metallic). They possess a long, broad scutellum (the triangular segment between their "shoulders."

Biology

Stink bugs, like their name implies, have well developed scent glands and can produce a bad odor. Primarily plant feeders (especially immature fruit and seeds) but a few species eat insects. Eggs laid in clusters on plants. They are typically barrel shaped and armed

This colorful nymph of the predacious stink bug *Apateticus cynicus* has captured a caterpillar and is feeding on it. Not all stink bugs are carnivores; in fact, most are plant feeders.

with spines. Females of many species protect their eggs and sometimes even the newly emerged young. Common spring and summer.

Banasa Stink Bug *Banasa dimidiata*

Watch for this very common stink bug on gooseberries and currants. Yellowish head, greenish thorax and abdomen and scutellum and reddish brown first pair of wings, although this coloration is variable. It is found on a variety of plants, especially berries. Found in spring and summer.

Dusky Stink Bug *Euschistus tristigmus*

Dark brown with light brown spots along edge of abdomen and a yellowish spot at the tip of the scutellum. Undersides are adorned with three (usually) spots down the midline; the "tri" in *tristigmus*. Watch for adults during the spring and summer.

Green Stink Bug *Acrosternum hilare*

Green Stink Bugs are green with yellow in the back of the head and along the edge of the abdomen. They are found on plants near wooded areas as well as gardens and orchards where they feed on the sap of many plants including fruit (*Prunus* spp. and *Amelanchier* sp.). Green Stink Bugs occur spring and summer.

Two-spotted Stink Bug *Cosmopepla lintneriana*

Goldenrod, columbine and mint, Hedge Nettle and Mullein are a few of the herbaceous plants this distinctive stink bug can be found on in weedy fields. Shiny black with two red spots on its scutellum. Active spring and summer. Formerly known as *Cosmopepla bimaculata*.

Stink Bug *Coenus delius*

Like the photo shows, this rounded stink bug is often found on grasses. The scutellum is more rounded, evenly merging with the wings than in other stink bugs. Also note the even coloration and myriad of tiny black pits.

Spined Soldier Bug *Podisus maculiventris*

Note the very pointed "shoulders" (front edge of prothorax) that give this bug its common name. Unlike most other stink bugs, a Spined Soldier Bug is predacious, feeding on a variety of insects, including leaf beetles and caterpillars (like this much larger Monarch caterpillar). Active May through July.

Parent Bugs
Family Acanthosomatidae

Appearance
Very similar to the pentatomid stink bugs.

Biology
Parent bugs are, indeed, very good parents. Once their barrel-shaped eggs hatch, the adults lead the nymphs to their feeding grounds.

Red-crossed Stink Bug *Elasmostethus cruciatus*

A northern stink bug that feeds on alder. Note the red **X** on the back that gives this stink bug its common name and Latin specific epithet, *cruciatus*. Found from April through September.

Parent Bug *Elasmucha lateralis*

This is the only North American *Elasmucha*. Adults and nymphs are commonly found on birch catkins and leaves. But the females lay their eggs elsewhere and lead the nymphs back to the birch where they feed. The female guards her brood of colorful nymphs, watching over them and hence the common name, "parent bug." One observer has noted the female flicking her wings at passing insects, presumably to scare them away. Some entomologists prefer to place this species with the stink bugs in family Pentatomidae.

Shield Bugs
Family Scutelleridae

Appearance

Very similar to stink bugs but with a "shield" that covers their entire back (actually an extension of the thorax).

Biology

One generation per year in the north. Overwinters as an adult.

Shield Bug *possibly Eurygaster species*

Both adults and nymphs have sucking mouthparts in which to pierce and feed on the juices of seeds, leaves and stems. One species, the Shieldbacked Pine Seed Bug (*Tetyra bipunctata*) feeds on the seeds of pine trees. Overwinters as an adult in the leaf litter and emerges in late spring through early summer.

Negro Bugs
Family Thyreocoridae

Appearance

Small, oval, black and shiny. Their scutellum is enlarged, covering the wings and most of the abdomen, giving them a beetle-like appearance.

Biology

Negro bugs are common on flowers, weeds and grasses in open fields.

Negro Bug *Corimelaena pulicaria*

A tiny bug with a hopelessly out-dated name. You may first assume that this is a tiny beetle, but notice that there is no line down the back where a beetle's wing covers would meet. Black with a pale edge to the corium (the thickened basal area of the front wing). Common on a wide variety of plants, including sunflowers. Active May through July.

Cicadas
Family Cicadidae

Appearance

Large, stout insects with green or brown bodies and black markings. Four membranous wings longer than the abdomen which they hold tent-like over their abdomens. Very short antennae between bulging eyes.

Biology

Cicadas insert eggs in tree twigs during late summer. Twigs wilt and drop. The nymphs hatch and tunnel into the ground where they remain feeding on the roots of trees for four to eight years. Adults start to emerge in July and are active into September. Cicadas are

A cicada emerges from its larval case.

well known for their ability to produce sound. The males use sound organs (tymbals) located on the sides of the base of their abdomen which vibrate and resonate into a cavity located inside parts of the thorax and abdomen. This produces a powerline type hum which is used to attract females. Each species creates its own unique sound.

Dogday Cicada *Tibicen canicularis*

Dogday Cicadas emerge every year and do not have a synchronized life cycle so we have cicadas emerging every year in the North Woods starting in July and August. The more "famous" Periodic Cicadas, which only emerge every 13 or 17 years, do not occur in the North Woods.

Cicada *Okanagana rimosa*

This northern cicada is smaller than the *Tibicen* Dogday Cicada above. Also note that the head is narrower than the thorax. Black marked with orange. The similar *Okanagana canadensis* is very patterned in black and orange underneath.

Acanaloniid Planthoppers
Family Acanaloniidae

Appearance
Often green with broad short wings held vertically, possibly to mimic a leaf.

Biology
Some consider this group to be a subfamily of Issidae called Acanaloniinae.

Two-striped Planthopper *Acanalonia bivittata*

A rather large and colorful species that can be common on shrubs. Can also occur in a delightful pink form. Mid July through September in the North Woods.

Flatid Planthoppers
Family Flatidae

Appearance
Small, between 1/5 to 1/2 inch long. They have short antennae positioned below the compound eyes. Moth-like with triangular, wedge-shaped wings held tent-like over the body.

Biology
They feed on trees, shrubs and vines gregariously in nonsocial groups.

Citrus Planthopper *Metcalfa pruinosa*

This lovely planthopper resembles a tiny moth. It is a light grayish blue to purplish. The color comes from whitish waxy bloom. Nymphs are even more thickly covered in wax. It feeds on the twigs of various woody plants. Adults are active during mid to late summer.

Treehoppers
Family Membracidae

Appearance

Small insects, most are between ⅕ to ⅓ inch long, with a large pronotum that extends back over the abdomen. The pronotum can assume a variety of different shapes, e.g. thorns and horns. Treehoppers are typically brown or green. Four membranous wings are partially exposed or hidden underneath the pronotum. The legs of treehoppers are all similarly sized with the hind legs slightly larger. Treehoppers possess very short, inconspicuous antennae.

Biology

Treehoppers are plant feeders, feeding on either trees and shrubs or herbaceous plants (some species will feed on herbaceous plants when immature and then woody plants as adults). Some treehoppers feed gregariously. Ants often tend certain species for their honeydew excretions. They have one or two generations a year. Treehoppers spend the winter as eggs inserted into plant tissue.

Treehopper *Ceresa basalis*

Ceresa basalis is an often encountered treehopper with a very broad pronotum. Color can vary wildly in this species but note the characteristic black body and face on top specimen. The dark legs, black undersides and brown patches on the sides of the pronotum, are distinctive. Willow is its food shrub.

Buffalo Treehopper *Ceresa alta*

Like its namesake, the Buffalo Treehopper has two "horns" sticking out of its pronotum (this name may be applied to other species). Also note the many pale spots and brownish tinge to the pronotum ridge. Eggs are laid in the twigs of hardwood trees, especially apple. They feed on both herbaceous plants and trees. Summer.

Treehopper *Entylia carinata*

Note this treehopper's unique "can opener" shape. An extremely variable species in its coloration. Often seen in summer on goldenrod and thistle stems. Very common in the North Woods.

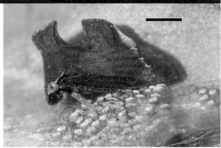

Treehopper *Telamona molaris*

The "molar"-like crest on this attractive treehopper is diagnostic; and it is the basis for its specific epithet, *molaris*. This species ranges north to Saskatchewan, Manitoba and Ontario.

Treehopper *Telamona monticola*

This common species is mainly found on oaks. It is mostly brown with some white markings on the pronotum. This treehopper is active in June.

Froghoppers (Spittlebugs) Family Cercopidae

Appearance

Small insects, most are between $1/5$ and $5/8$ inch long. The back legs are enlarged for jumping. Froghoppers are recognized by the circle of short spines on the hind leg. They have short antennae located between their compound eyes. Their forewings are longer than their abdomen, are leathery and held tent-like over their body. The hindwings are large and membranous. Most froghoppers are brown or gray, although a few are dark with red markings.

Biology

Froghoppers feed on the plant sap from primarily herbaceous plants and occasionally trees and shrubs. The immature nymphs are better known as spittlebugs. They have the ability to create a frothy mass around their body by mixing air with a fluid secreted from the anus which creates bubbles. They use this froth to protect themselves from drying out and from predators and parasitoids. Froghoppers overwinter as eggs inserted into plant stems.

This is the "spittle" that the nymphs create by mixing air with a fluid secreted from their anus. It deters predators and parasitoids.

This is a nymph taken from the spittle.

Pine Spittlebug *Aphrophora parallela*

Look for this appropriately-named spittlebug on White Pine, Scotch Pine and Jack Pine. It is grayish brown with scattered dark and light spots. Eggs hatch in the spring. Adult Pine Spittlebugs are active July and August.

Diamond-backed Spittlebug *Lepyronia quadrangularis*

Its hard to tell which end is which with this angular spittle-bug. Like their name implies, Diamond-backed Spittlebugs have a dark outline of a diamond shape when viewed from above.

Meadow Spittlebug *Philaenus spumarius*

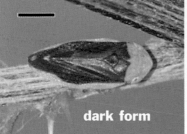

dark form

Two variations of this common spittlebug are shown above; One is dark with a light edging and the other has several large white blotches. Many color forms exist. This species is the creator of much of the spittle masses we see on plants. It was introduced from Europe.

Leafhoppers
Family Cicadellidae

Appearance

Small slender insects, most are between ¹/₈ and ¹/₂ inch long. Leafhoppers have large back legs that have a row of small spines on lower part of the hind legs. They are typically green or brown, although some are brightly colored. They have short antennae located between their compound eyes. Their forewings are leathery while their hindwings are membranous.

Biology

Leafhoppers are plant feeders on a wide range of trees, shrubs and herbaceous plants. They can go through more than one generation a year. They lay eggs into plant tissue. Most leafhoppers overwinter as eggs or adults, although there are some species that are carried into the North Woods on air currents.

Fourspotted Clover Leafhopper *Agallia quadripunctata*

Look for the four spots on the head and pronotum that give this leafhopper its common and Latin names (sometimes only two are visible). Also note the unique wing markings—light colored veins against a dark background. It is known to feed on elm. Look for this leafhopper from May to August.

Silver Leafhopper *Athysansus argentarius*

The Silver Leafhopper is an immigrant from Europe that has spread across North America. It is quite common and often on alfalfa (though this specimen was photographed on a milkweed). Light colored with dark colored veins. They are common from June to August.

Striped Leafhopper   *Cuerna striata*

When you first see this leafhopper up close, you will likely say "wow!" The colors are stunning. Also note in this photo, the hitchhiking red mite on the leafhopper's back. Congregations of adults overwinter together. The large black head and prothorax, give it a toe-headed appearance. Commonly found on thistles, May through September.

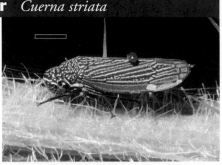

Candy-striped Leafhopper   *Graphocephala coccinea*

Quite common, the Candy-striped Leafhopper is also quite beautiful. It is red and green/blue with a yellow head and legs. It is found in fields and the edge of wooded areas. Candy-striped leafhoppers feed on blackberry (*Ribes* sp.) and a variety of other plants. Watch for them during mid to late summer.

Grape Leafhopper   *Erythroneura comes*

A beautiful pest of grape plants, the Grape Leafhopper lays its eggs inside the leaf. Nymphs feed on the underside of the leaves sucking out cell liquids, eventually damaging the leaf. If enough leafhoppers are present the grapes themselves could be damaged with increased acidity and lower sugar content. May to October.

Eight-lined Leafhopper   *Gyponana octolineata*

A relatively large leafhopper that sometimes comes to lights. Normally green, there are also pink and pink-marked color morphs. May carry plant diseases such as aster yellows.

Aphids
Family Aphididae

Appearance

Very small, $1/25$ to $1/5$ inch long, soft-bodied pear-shaped insects. They possess long antennae and a pair of tube-like structures on the abdomen called cornicles. Aphids occur in many colors including green, red, yellow, orange, black, and gray. Most aphids are wingless, although some possess four membranous wings.

Biology

All aphids are plant feeders, feeding on essentially all types of woody and herbaceous plants. They usually overwinter as eggs which hatch into females. They aphids reproduce parthenogenetically, i.e. eggs develop without being fertilized.

Winged and wingless adults are often found feeding together as in this group of Brown Ambrosia Aphids.

The eggs hatch inside the females and are born live. Several generations can be produced like this. These individuals are wingless. Eventually winged individuals are formed which will fly to alternate plant hosts. During late summer, a generation of reproductive males and females are formed. They mate and females lay eggs which remain until the following spring. Aphids produce honeydew, a sugary sticky waste material. Honeydew can be a food source of other insects, especially ants.

Oleander Aphid *Aphis nerii*

Oleander Aphids enliven milkweed stems in spring and summer. They are orange with black legs and cornicles. They feed on milkweeds by taking in sugary stem sap from beaks embedded in the stem. Introduced species.

Brown Ambrosia Aphid *Uroleucon ambrosiae*

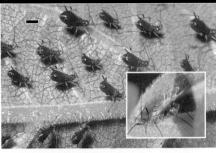

Like with most aphid species, you will often find wingless Brown Ambrosia Aphids and those with wings together on a plant, often *Rudbeckia*, coneflower and sunflower (see photo on opposite page). Also note the tiny drop of liquid on the tips of some of their long, thin, black cornicles. This is a defensive liquid. While this aphid can be found throughout the spring and summer, it is particularly noticeably from mid to late summer.

Greater Striped Red Oak Aphid *Myzocallis bellus*

A huge name for a tiny insect; The Greater Striped Red Oak Aphid, not surprisingly, feeds on a variety of trees, especially red and black oak. It is yellowish with two rows of black spots on its abdomen and black veined wings. It is found throughout the spring and summer.

Woolly Alder Aphid *Paraprociphilus tessellatus*

White fuzzy masses on Speckled Alder stems in the North Woods may be a dense congregation of Woolly Alder Aphids. The "wool" is actually long strands of a waxy secretion that discourages predators and helps insulate the insects from water loss.

Booklice & Barklice
Order Psocoptera

Diversity
There are 23 families and about 340 species in North America. Psocids are common in the North Woods.

Appearance
Adults: Psocids are small, most are less than 1/4 inch long, and soft-bodied insects. They are generally colored gray or brown, although a few can be brightly colored. Most psocids (barklice) possess four membranous wings which are held roof-like over their bodies. The forewings are a little larger than the hind wings. Some psocids (booklice) lack wings. Psocids have moderately long antennae, chewing mouthparts and an enlarged, bulb-like clypeus (nose).

Nymphs:The immature nymphs are very similar to adults but are smaller and lack wings.

Habitats
Many psocids (barklice) are found outdoors on or under bark, on tree and shrub leaves and under stones or dead leaves. Some species live inside buildings (booklice) where they are found associated with books and paper.

Life cycle
Psocids develop using paurometabolous metamorphosis, a type of simple metamorphosis. Some species cover their eggs with silk.

Food
Barklice feed on fungi, lichen, pollen, decaying plants and other organic material. Booklice feed on molds as well as fungi, grains, insect fragments and other starchy material, including glue from book bindings.

What's In a Name
Despite being called barklice and booklice, psocids do not resemble head lice and other true lice nor are related to them. Psocids do not bite people and are harmless to humans.

Don't confuse them with...
...members of the Hemiptera, especially froghoppers, treehoppers and leafhoppers. These insects have piercing-sucking mouthparts, have short antennae and lack a conspicuous clypeus (nose). Barklice may be confused for true lice. True lice have short antennae, lack a conspicuous clypeus (nose) and are parasitic on animals.

Barklouse   *Cerastipsocus venosus*

Often found on the trunks of maples where it feeds on lichens, fungi, etc. "Herds" of nymphs may feed alongside adults. Note the long antennae, contrastingly marked wing veins and chewing mouthparts to separate them from similar aphids and psyllids. A beautiful insect when viewed closely. Photographed in early September.

Barklouse   *Psocus leidyi*

Commonly found on standing dead trees, and often on White Pine (*Pinus strobus*). Note the black "nose," black dots on the thorax and the three black spots across the middle of the forewing that clinch the identification of this barklouse. Males have larger eyes than females. Photographed in late September.

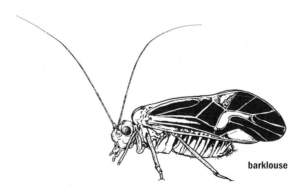

barklouse

Beetles
Order Coleoptera

Diversity
This is the most abundant group of insects for total number of species. Roughly 40 percent of all insects are beetles! There are as many beetles as there all plant species combined. There are 128 families and about 30,000 species in North America.

Appearance
Adults: Beetles are generally elongate, cylindrical, or hemispherical in shape. Most are black or brown, although there are many that brightly colored. Beetles have four wings. They are distinguished from other insects by the first pair, called elytra, which are hardened or leathery and typically cover the abdomen. The second pair of wings are membranous and used for flight. Beetles possess well developed mandibles and have chewing mouthparts. The antennae are quite variable in form and size. Species range from very small, $1/20^{th}$ inch to large, three inches long.

Larvae: Beetle larvae generally have conspicuous heads and elongate and flattened bodies, although others can be worm-like, cylindrical, or curled into a C-shaped body. Most beetle larvae possess legs although a few species lack them.

Habitats
Beetles are found in essentially all habitats in the North Woods, including terrestrial sites, e.g forests and prairies. They occupy open areas, are found on flowers, in fungi, on carrion, in the leaf litter and even under bark or in the wood of trees and shrubs. Some beetles are subterranean. Others are found in aquatic or semiaquatic areas.

Life Cycle
Beetles are holometabolous insects, going through complete metamorphosis to develop. Most beetles take one year to go through their life cycle once. Some beetles, particularly those living in wood or soil can take more than one year, some as long as seven years. Other beetles can complete more than one generation in a year.

Food
Very diverse. Many beetles are plant feeders, feeding on essentially all plant parts, including leaves, fruits, flower blossoms, roots, branches and trunks. Others are predaceous, especially on other insects. Yet others

are scavengers on decaying animal or plant matter while others are fungus feeders. Some beetles feed on a range of foods while others are very specialized.

Sound Production
Many beetles produce sound, especially by stridulation, i.e. rubbing different body parts together. In many cases, beetles produce sounds for defensive reasons.

Don't confuse them with...
...true bugs. You can distinguish between them as true bugs have hemelytrous wings and needle-like mouthparts.

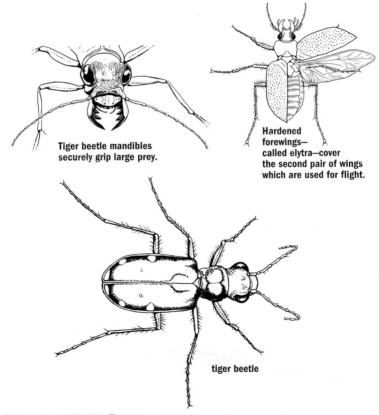

Tiger beetle mandibles securely grip large prey.

Hardened forewings—called elytra—cover the second pair of wings which are used for flight.

tiger beetle

Ground Beetles & Tiger Beetles Family Carabidae

Appearance

Small to moderate sized beetles, generally between ⅛ to ½ inches long with flattened bodies and parallel sided wing covers. The head is narrower than the pronotum with moderate length thread-like antennae. These beetles possess long, slender legs with a large trochanter on each of the last pair of legs. They are generally black or brown, although some are brightly colored, including blue, green, or red. This group of beetles contains the third largest number of beetle species in North America.

A tiger beetle larva waits for prey in its circular burrow in the sand.

Biology

Ground beetles are active at night and are occasionally attracted to lights. They hide during the day and are typically found on the ground under leaves, logs, stones, loose bark, in grassy areas, although a few can be found in trees. When exposed, ground beetles typically

Tiger beetles were formerly placed in their own family (Cicindelidae).

move quickly to find shelter but rarely fly. Tiger beetles, however, are active during the day and are usually found in sunny areas. Ground beetles and tiger beetles are predaceous, feeding on other insects as well as other invertebrate animals. Some species are scavengers and a few eat seeds. You can find ground beetles during spring and summer.

Fiery Hunter *Calosoma calidum*

The Fiery Hunter is named for its iridescent rows of red and gold punctures along the wing covers. Hunts for prey strictly on the ground. It is found in fields, open woodlands and on beaches. Its colorful cousin the Caterpillar Hunter (*C. scrutator*) has a green elytra and a purple pronotum rimmed with red. Searches for caterpillars on beaches, in gardens, in fields but usually close to deciduous woods.

Searcher *Carabus maeander*

This Searcher is associated with marshes and small lakes—photo was taken on a gravel woodland path near a stream. Iridescent dark wing covers are interrupted by elytra ridges and welts. A reddish margin along the border of its prothorax and wing covers is always present. It is commonly found from May through August.

Pedunculate Ground Beetle *Scarites quadriceps*

A distinctive ground beetle because of the pronounced space between its pronotum and wing covers. Shiny black. Also note the large mandibles. Typically found in or near weedy fields and agricultural fields where they burrow under leaf litter and other debris into the soil. Sometimes near beaches.

Minute Ground Beetle *Bembidion confusum*

Bare shorelines, mudflats and wet beaches are the preferred haunts of *Bembidion* species. This truly minute species is shiny coppery brown. North America is home to over 250 species of *Bembidion*. Common during June and July.

Colorful Foliage Ground Beetle *Lebia species*

The name says it all; It is colorful (red and blue), found on foliage (flowers too) and in the ground beetle family. Colorful Foliage Ground Beetles are good climbers and are typically found on flowers and foliage where they eat aphids. Note that the head is constricted into a "neck" behind the eyes.

Woodland Ground Beetle *Agonum cupripenne*

Note the very oval body and the iridescent green head and prothorax. The wing covers are a reddish purplish color with a rim of green around the edges. You can find this beetle spring and summer.

Woodland Ground Beetle *Agonum placidum*

Unlike related woodland ground beetles that are found near water, this beetle is found in dry fields and woods. It is uniformly shiny black. There are many *Agonum* species but *A. placidum* is one of the most common.

Woodland Ground Beetle *Poecilus chalcites*

A farmer's best friend? *Poecilus chalcites* has been recognized as a valuable biological control agent, predating on crop pests early in the growing season. It is iridescent green or bronze (although sometimes it can appear black). The prothorax has several indented areas. Commonly found under rocks, boards and logs.

Vivid Metallic Ground Beetle *Chlaenius sericeus*

Normally a vivid iridescent green in the right light; but sometimes reddish (photo) or with bluish tinges. Fine, short silky hairs on its wing covers. Will emit a pungent odor if alarmed. Found along the margins of lakes and streams. It lays eggs in mud balls which it attaches to plants. It is common for them to eat larger insects that are injured or already dead.

Laurentian Tiger Beetle *Cicindela denikei*

A very boreal and very rare tiger beetle. *Cicindela denikei* is listed as Threatened in Minnesota. At first glance it may seem very similar to the Six-spotted Tiger Beetle, but this species has no spots and is found north of the Six-spotted's range. Found on rock slabs in its limited range: northern Minnesota adjacent to southeast Manitoba and northwest Ontario.

Twelve-spotted Tiger Beetle *Cicindela duodecimguttata*

Vertical river banks or lake shores are particularly attractive to this species. Elytral markings are often reduced to spots (though, you may have to use your imagination to see twelve distinct spots!).

Beautiful Tiger Beetle *Cicindela formosa*

Formosa in Latin means "beautiful." Bold cream-colored maculations edge the deep reddish purple elytra. Found along the sand dunes of Lake Superior and Lake Michigan; Also in dry sandy upland sites like old gravel pits. This is a spring/fall species.

Ghost Tiger Beetle *Cicindela lepida*

Ghost Tiger Beetles are a perfect match to their white-sand environs; They often blend so perfectly with the beach sands that they are nearly invisible—some would say "ghost-like." Most easily found by looking for their shadow! Found on Great Lakes sandy beaches and other vegetation-free sand pits. Summer species with a two-year life cycle.

Green-margined Tiger Beetle *Cicindela limbalis*

Green rims the abdomen contrasting with the purplish-red elytra. Clay soils; steep river banks, road cuts, hill tops. Also called the Claybank Tiger Beetle. Spring/fall species (April to July and August to September) with a three-year life cycle.

Boreal Long-lipped Tiger Beetle *Cicindela longilabris*

A real northerner, the Long-lipped Tiger Beetle is found near bogs on gravel roads, sandy trails and rocks in the boreal regions. It appears black and has a contrasting white "lip." Light markings on the elytra are thin and inconspicuous. Spring/fall species that can be found May to September.

Backroad Tiger Beetle *Cicindela punctulata*

Maybe the most urban of our tiger beetles, *Cicindela punctulata* can be found on sunny sidewalks if there is grass nearby. But quite common in natural environments too, and often associated with *C. formosa* and *C. scutellaris*. Note the row of green punctures running down the length of each elytra; This is visible in the field.

Cow Path Tiger Beetle *Cicindela purpurea*

Maybe you will see this species along a cow path, as long as it is in fairly open grassland. Also found in openings in clay soil habitats. Greenish or purplish iridescence and limited elytral light markings. Similar to *Cicindela limbalis* but no light spots on shoulder. April to June and August to October.

Bronzed Tiger Beetle *Cicindela repanda repanda*

Probably the most abundant tiger beetle in the North Woods. Usually found near water: beaches, sand bars, mud flats, river banks. This is a spring/fall species with a two-year life cycle. Adults found April to July and again August to October. The Beach Tiger Beetle (*C. hirticollis*) is larger and the shoulder marks are coat-hook shaped.

Festive Tiger Beetle *Cicindela scutellaris lecontei*

Festive indeed, this tiger beetle varies in color from iridescent dark green (bottom photo) to reddish purple (top photos). A cream colored band edges the margins of the wing covers but also can be broken in several spots (bottom photo). Festive Tiger Beetles are found in dry, sandy areas, especially amongst stands of pines. April through September.

Six-spotted Tiger Beetle *Cicindela sexguttata*

Despite its name, the number of white spots on its iridescent green elytra are variable from zero to eight (six on the specimen photographed). It is found in deciduous forests and adjacent open areas and is particularly common on gravel roads, sunny trails, logs and stones. Six-spotted Tiger Beetles are very active during the day, moving quickly in short bursts. They spend the winter as adults in their larval tunnels. Adults are out and about from May into July.

Whirligig Beetles
Family Gyrinidae

Appearance

Moderate sized beetles, $1/8$ to $5/8$ inch long. They are dark-colored, elongate oval, and somewhat flattened beetles. The first pair of legs are long and slender while the second and third pairs of legs are short and inconspicuous. They have two pairs of compound eyes and short clubbed antennae.

Biology

Whirligig beetles swim in groups on the surface of ponds and streams, moving in a crisscrossing, seemingly random pattern. How do they avoid each other? They sense and react to the ripples

Large groups of Whirligig Beetles can be found in quiet waters.

made by the other beetles. They can dive below the surface if necessary. They are able to see above and below the surface of the water simultaneously. Whirligig beetles are opportunistic, feeding on small insects that have fallen into water. They overwinter as adults and lay their eggs on the underside of the leaves of aquatic plants.

Large Whirligig Beetle *Dineutus species*

These are the small beetles that make crazy loop-the-loops on the surface of lakes, ponds and streams—often in large groups (see photo above). Large whirligig beetles are generally black, although some may appear bronzed. Their wings covers are smooth or with nine faint grooves while their scutellum is hidden. Adults overwinter in mud or on plants in the water and are active spring and summer.

Predaceous Diving Beetles Family Dytiscidae

Appearance

Elongate oval, convex beetles that are moderate in size, most measuring between ³/16 to 1¹/2 inches long. They are generally dark-colored, although they are sometimes yellowish, or have light colored markings. The antennae are thread-like and moderate in length. The back pair of legs are flattened and fringed with hair.

Biology

Predaceous diving beetles live in ponds, lakes, and streams. They are good swimmers, moving their hind legs in unison. They float at the surface of water, their head pointed down. They store air underneath their wing covers which allows them to swim underwater for a long time. Predaceous diving beetles feed on other insects and other small creatures, including small fish. They typically overwinter as larvae burrowed into the mud at the bottom of the water. Eggs are laid on aquatic plants or dropped loose into the water. They pupate in earthen cells on shore.

Predaceous Diving Beetle *Dytiscus species*

Like mini scuba tanks, these beetles store air beneath their wing covers to use during extended dives. Though an aquatic beetle, the predaceous diving beetle is occasionally seen at night near homes where they've been attracted to lights. These are large predaceous diving beetles with yellow edging on the wing covers and pronotum. The distinctive larva are known as "water tigers," and they are efficient predators of aquatic critters including small fish. Adults are active in April as well as June and July.

larva

Water Scavenger Beetles
Family Hydrophilidae

Appearance

Elongate oval, somewhat convex beetles, water scavenger beetles are small to large in size, with most species measuring between $^1/_{16}$ to $^5/_8$ inches long. Water scavenger beetles possess short, clubbed antennae with slender palps that are as long or longer than the antennae. Their hind legs are flattened and fringed with hair. Aquatic species are distinctive because of a long spine running down the middle on the underside of their body.

Biology

Nearly all water scavenger beetles are aquatic living in ponds and lakes (there is small group of water scavenger beetles that are terrestrial, living in dung). Unlike the predaceous diving beetles, water scavenger beetles swim with their hind legs moving alternately. They can carry a film of air on the underside of their body when they swim under water. Most water scavenger beetles are scavengers, feeding on decaying plant debris. There are a few species that are predaceous, preying on aquatic invertebrates.

Giant Water Scavenger Beetle *Hydrophilus triangularis*

This large shiny black beetle is common in weedy ponds as well as streams. It can be common flying to lights at night. It feeds on live or dead small aquatic animals. A Giant Water Scavenger Beetle is commonly found during summer.

Clown Beetles
Family Histeridae

Appearance

Small, broadly oval and very convex beetles generally no more than ³/₈ inch long. They possess short, clubbed elbowed antennae. Their elytra are short and squared off, exposing one or two abdominal segments. The tibia of the first pair of legs are expanded with teeth or spines. They are typically black, sometimes with red markings.

Biology

Clown beetles are found associated with decaying organic matter, such as dung, dead animals, plants, and rotting fungi, as well as sap where they feed on soft-bodied larvae and eggs, especially of flies. They can also be associated with ant nests and animal burrows.

Clown Beetle *Saprinus species*

Look around around animal carcasses and dung for these clown beetles; This is where they feed on fly larvae (maggots) and fly eggs. The *Saprinus* clown beetles are shiny black with grooves in the wing covers. They can retract their antennae into grooves underneath the pronotum. They are common May to July.

Carrion Beetles
Family Silphidae

Appearance

Elongate to broadly oval and generally flattened beetles, carrion beetles are moderate sized with many over 1/2 inch long. The antennae are moderate length and clubbed. They can be long, covering the abdomen or short and squared off, exposing part of the abdomen. Many carrion beetles are black or black with orange or red markings while a few are black and yellow.

Biology

Carrion beetles are typically associated with dead animals, while others are found on dung or decaying plant matter. Some species bury small, freshly deceased animals they find, providing their young with food. This strategy reduces competition with flies that also seek out dead animals. Other carrion beetles are attracted to carcasses that have been dead longer and have started to dry out which also reduces competition with necrophorous flies.

A dead White-tailed Deer is irresistible to Margined Carrion Beetles. They are often seen mating on such carcasses, the male holding on to the female until she lays her eggs.

Carrion Beetle *Heterosilpha ramosa*

Road-killed deer are a favorite of *Heterosilpha ramosa* and can become quite abundant near them. It favors larger carcasses where it feeds on fly maggots.

American Carrion Beetle *Necrophila americana*

American Carrion Beetles are broadly oval insects. They have a black head with a mustard yellow pronotum with a large black blotch in the center. The wrinkly-looking wing covers are blackish with a little yellow on the posterior tip. In flight they can be mistaken for bumble bees. American Carrion Beetles feed on drying carcasses as well

as fly and beetle larvae. They are common from June through August.

Burying Beetle (Sexton Beetle) *Nicrophorus species*

Burying beetles dig shallow pits to bury freshly killed animals. It's not morbid, its just the life of a Burying Beetle. They then mate and lay eggs on the carcass. Adult protect the larvae while they feed and develop. Burying beetles are black with orange markings on their wing covers. The wing covers seem to short for their abdomen, leaving sev-

eral segments exposed. Burying Beetles are common from June through August.

Margined Carrion Beetle *Oiceoptoma noveboracense*

Like many members of the Silphidae, this species is often seen in pairs in mating position; The male on top of the female, holding her antennae in his jaw. He will hold her until she has laid her eggs. It is black with pinkish orange along the margin of the pronotum behind the head. It is common in forested areas and is active May to August. Often seen at lights at night.

Rove Beetles
Family Staphylinidae

Appearance

Slender, flat beetles ranging considerably in size from ¹/₁₆ to one inch long. Vast majority of species are tiny. They are conspicuous because their elytra are very short, exposing most of the abdomen which is flexible. Rove beetles have fully developed hind wings which they fold underneath the short elytra. Most rove beetles are blackish or brownish. This is largest group of beetles in North America.

Biology

Rove beetles are found in many types of habitats, especially decaying organic material, including dead animals and dung. They are also associated with fungus and found on the ground under stones, leaves, loose bark and along shorelines. Most rove beetles are nocturnal and are predaceous on other insects.

Hairy Rove Beetle   *Creophilus maxillosus*

The Hairy Rove Beetle is somewhat hairy, black and with golden yellow bands on its wing covers and abdomen. It is associated with dead animals where it feeds on fly maggots. It is common from June to August.

Rove Beetle   *Platydracus cinnamopterus*

This adult rove beetle has a reddish head and wing covers. The abdomen is black with some red. It feeds on insects in finds in soil and other habitats. Look for this rove beetle from April into June.

Stag Beetles
Family Lucanidae

Appearance

Elongate oval medium to large beetles, with most measuring between ½ to one inch long. They have short antennae that end in three asymmetrical lobes. They are not able to hold these terminal segments together. Males particularly have large mandibles. Stag beetles are black or dark brown, though a few species are iridescent blue or green.

Biology

Stag beetles are usually associated with trees because the larvae inhabit the decaying wood of stumps and logs of both hardwood and evergreen trees. Adults feed on sap that exudes from plants. They lay their eggs into the cracks and crevices of bark or logs. Stag beetles are often attracted to lights at night.

Stag Beetle   *Lucanus placidus*

This stag beetle species emerges in May or June, sometimes in large numbers. It isn't uncommon for them to emerge from the ground when they develop in old, decaying tree roots. This stag species is a little larger than one inch in size, is reddish to dark brown in color. They are associated with hardwood trees, including oak.

Earth-boring Dung Beetles
Family Geotrupidae

Appearance

Oval, convex stout beetles, measuring $3/16$ to one inch long with wing covers covering their abdomen. They are typically black or dark brown.

Biology

They are typically found in and around dung while some are associated with carrion, rotting wood, or fungi. They construct tunnels for the larvae, sometimes as long as several feet which is provisioned with dung or plant material.

Earth-boring Dung Beetle *Geotrupes splendidus*

Start poking around cow poop if you want a peak at this good looking beetle with a metallic bronze, purple or green sheen. It is found in pastures with cattle dung, beneath which it constructs a fairly shallow tunnel, about one foot deep, in which the female will lay eggs. You can find this species throughout the spring and summer.

Scarab Beetles
Family Scarabaeidae

Appearance

A large and variable group of beetles. They range from small to large, most between 1/4 to one inch long. They are slender to broadly oval and heavy bodied. Most scarabs are generally convex. They possess short antennae that usually end with three asymmetrical lobes. Unlike stag beetles, scarab beetles can compress these lobes into a club or fan them out to detect smells. Many scarab beetles are dark-colored, black or brown, but some are more brightly colored orange, gold or green.

Biology

Their habits are quite varied. Many are scavengers feeding on a variety of decaying organic matter while others feed on dung. Some feed on plants, including leaves and fruit and some feed on pollen. A few are fungus feeders and a few even live in the burrows or nests of animals. Many scarabs take one year to complete their life cycle but there are some species than can take three years. Look for them at lights at night.

Dung Beetle *Onthophagus hecate*

Like a miniature rhino, males have a horn on the pronotum. The middle and hind tibia of the legs are expanded. This dung beetle is dull black. Dung beetles are found around mammal dung where they will dig a hole under the feces for the larvae. Look for these dung beetles from May to July.

June Beetle *Phyllophaga species*

Who doesn't have a somewhat creepy memory of june beetles whirring at the screen door after dark? But they were simply attracted to the lights during their night flights in May and June. They sound like huge bumble bees when flying. June beetles feed on the leaves of hardwood trees, such as oak, ash, birch and willow. They have a two to three year life cycle with the larvae, called white grubs, spending their time in the soil.

Rose Chafer *Macrodactylus subspinosus*

Rose Chafers are commonly found on flower blossoms, especially (not surprisingly) roses, as well as fruit, including grapes, and the leaves of many different trees, shrubs and other plants. They have orangish spiny legs. Active June through July and are found particularly in areas with sandy soil.

Chafer *Dichelonyx subvittata*

This slender beetle is brownish with an iridescent greenish sheen. There is a dark stripe on each wing cover, although this can be indistinct. The Chafer is found on oaks, where it feeds on the leaves. Adults are found in May and June.

Japanese Beetle *Popillia japonica*

The five white side brushes of hair are distinctive on this introduced species. Native to Japan, it was accidentally brought to the East Coast a century ago, eventually reaching the North Woods. Common in landscapes and gardens where it feeds on over 300 species, including rose, grape and linden. Late June into September.

Sand Chafer (False Japanese Beetle) *Strigoderma arbicola*

Sand Chafers overwinter as larvae in the soil and adults are active for several weeks starting in late June or early July. They are only found in areas with sandy soil. Sand Chafers commonly feed on the blossoms of many plants but may also feed on foliage and fruit of various plants.

Grape Pelidnota *Pelidnota punctata*

Grape Pelidnotas are brownish tan with six black spots along the edge of the wing covers and two black spots on the prothorax. They feed on grape leaves (when available) during May and June. They are also attracted to lights.

Goldsmith Beetle *Cotalpa lanigera*

The impressive Goldsmith Beetle is uniformly a yellowish cream color. The prothorax typically has an iridescent green sheen. Look for it in woods and sandy streamside habitats. It feeds on the leaves of willow, poplar and oak and is active May and June.

Hairy Flower Scarab *Trichiotinus assimilis & T. piger*

These bee mimics are a common sight on flowers in June and July. Hairy is right; Long creamy yellow colored hairs cover the body. This flower beetle has a black head and prothorax. The wing covers are black and brown with two white stripes at right angles on each wing cover and two white stripes down the center of the wing covers. The two species (*T. assimilis* and *T. piger)* are very similar.

Metallic Wood-boring Beetles
Family Buprestidae

Appearance

Small to moderate sized beetles, most are between ⅛ to one inch long. They are bullet to elongate oval shaped beetles and flattened. The head is somewhat retracted into the prothorax with moderate length antennae. They are iridescent or metallic with many colored bronze, black, or green with some with yellow or red markings.

Biology

Metallic wood boring beetles are typically borers in deciduous trees and shrubs. A few species occur in other plants, including evergreens and berries. They generally overwinter as larvae under the bark. Adults emerge in spring and lay eggs on trunks or branches. Adults feed on the leaves of the host plant. Some may also be found on flowers where they feed on pollen.

Divergent Metallic Wood Borer *Dicerca divaricata*

As pretty as a piece of gold jewelry, this metallic wood-boring beetle is iridescent gold and sculptured. The tip of the wing covers noticeably narrow to short "tails" that slightly diverge (hence the specific epithet). They lay their eggs in a variety of dead and dying hardwood trees. They are commonly seen May and June.

Yellow-marked Metallic Wood Borer
Acmaeodera pulchella

This metallic wood-boring beetle species is black with yellow markings, and somewhat teardrop shaped. Flying with wing covers closed, they are convincing wasp mimics. They attack pine and are found on flowers during June and July.

Emerald Ash Borer *Agrilus planipennis*

Native to China, Mongolia, Korea and Japan, the Emerald Ash Borer was first discovered in North America in southeast Michigan in 2002. Since then it has spread to the North Woods in the U.P. of Michigan. As of July 2009 it had been found in all counties in Michigan, two counties in southeast Wisconsin, two counties in southwest Wisconsin and one county in Minnesota. Expect to find this insect in additional sites in the North Woods in the near future. Its range expansion does not bode well for our northern ashes (*Fraxinus* species). The larvae tunnel under the bark, eventually killing the trees. Emerald Ash Borers are active from late May through August.

Bronze Birch Borer *Agrilus anxius*

This native species only becomes a serious problem to birches (*Betula* species) when other stressors such as drought and age already affects the trees. This is what happened to the Paper Birch forests of the North Shore of Lake Superior after a long drought in the 1990s. You can still see large stands of standing dead trees. The larvae tunnel underneath the bark. Active late May into early July.

Red-necked Cane Borer *Agrilus ruficollis*

Who you callin' a "redneck?" Red necked Cane Borers have a coppery-red prothorax ("neck") and iridescent bluish black wing covers. They feed on the leaves of raspberries and blackberries and girdle the tips of canes to lay eggs. Look for Red-necked Cane Borers on the foliage of plants June through August.

Click Beetles
Family Elateridae

Appearance

Small to moderate sized beetles, they are typically between $1/8$ to $1/2$ inch long (one species is up to $13/4$ inches long). They are elongate oval and flattened beetles and are typically dark brown or black. The prothorax appears "loose" from the rest of the body. The back corners of the prothorax are prolonged into sharp points. Click beetles have moderate length antennae.

Biology

Click beetles are found on foliage and flowers as well as under bark. Some species are predaceous on aphids while others feed on pollen, nectar and decaying fruit. A click beetle is unique because it can right itself when it is on its back. It arches the area between the prothorax and mesothorax and then snaps it back (usually producing an audible "click"). If it fails the first time, it will keep trying until it succeeds. Click beetles commonly are attracted to lights. The larvae are commonly called wireworms and can take five to seven years to develop.

Click Beetle *Agriotes fucosus*

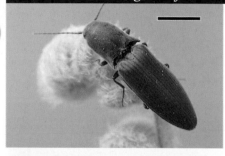

Agriotes fucosus is blackish with reddish brown around the lateral margins of its pronotum. It is associated with woodland vegetation (this one photographed on a fern along a woodland path). They have a pronotum that is long as wide. These click beetles are active from May through July.

Click Beetle *Melanotus species*

These click beetles are typically brown and have a pronotum that is longer than it is wide. Identification is tricky; 51 species in North America. Look for these click beetles from May through July

Eyed Click Beetle *Alaus oculatus*

Who's watching who? Eyed Click Beetles are large and conspicuous, sporting two large velvety black eye spots surrounded by a gray ring on their dark gray pronotum. The wing covers are black mottled with small whitish patches. Eyed Click Beetles are associated with decaying logs and stumps and are found in open wooded areas. They are active in May and June.

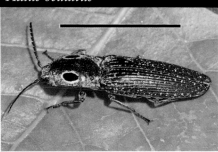

Net-winged Beetles
Family Lycidae

Appearance
Moderate sized beetles, generally about ¼ to ½ inch long. They have soft wing covers with raised ridges. The wing covers are fan-shaped and soft. The head is partially hidden underneath the pronotum. Many net-winged beetles are black, although some can be brightly colored orange or red. They have moderately long antennae with broad, flat segments.

Biology
Net-winged beetles are often associated with wooded areas and are common on foliage, flowers, and trees. They feed on other insects as well as juices from decaying plants, nectar and honeydew. Net-winged beetles are distasteful to potential predators and they apparently do not have any known natural enemies.

End Band Net-wing Beetle *Calopteron terminale*

At first glance, it would be easy to mistake a net-winged beetle for a moth. But the colorful "wings" are actually wing covers. It has a bluish black head and prothorax. Wing covers are orange with the posterior third bluish black. They are found during August and September on foliage and flowers.

Fireflies (Lightning Bugs) Family Lampyridae

Appearance

Flattened beetles with soft wing covers, often with orangish, yellowish or reddish markings on their pronotum. The head is generally hidden underneath the pronotum.

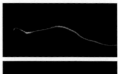

Biology

Fireflies are associated with damp areas on foliage. Some adult fireflies are predacious, while others feed on pollen and nectar. Fireflies produce light (bioluminescence) on the tip of abdomen on the underside. Oxygen combines with a chemical called luciferin producing luciferase. This bioluminescence is used to communicates to members of the opposite sex through a series of light flashes at night, each species creating a unique pattern. Not all fireflies can produce light, especially the smaller species.

Larval fireflies are well-protected predators of snails, slugs and worms.

Different species produce different light flash patterns and colors (top). It is the tip of the abdomen that bioluminesces.

Winter Firefly *Ellychnia corrusca*

Contrary to its common name, this species lacks the ability to produce light as an adult. And unlike other fireflies, it is active during the day. It has blackish to olive wing covers and a black pronotum with a ring of pinkish red. It is found on tree trunks, foliage and flowers (like asters) from May through August.

Black Firefly *Lucidota atra*

A day-active flyer, this firefly species has slate black wing covers and a pronotum that is black in the center, reddish to orange along side the center and pale yellow to orange around the edges. Lucidota atra is commonly spotted from May through July.

Firefly *Photuris pennsylvanica*

After dark on warm summer nights watch for the greenish flashes of *Photuris* species. This nocturnal firefly has slate black wing covers with three dull yellow stripes. The pronotum is mostly black with some dull yellow and pinkish red markings. They are in found in fields and open woods during May through July.

Dermestid Beetles
Family Dermestidae

Appearance

Small beetles, measuring between ¹/₁₆ to ¹/₂ inch long. They are usually convex oval to elongate oval beetles. Their wing covers are often covered with hair or scales. They have short, clubbed antennae. Most are black and brown, although a few can have interestingly colored patterns.

Biology

Dermestid beetles are scavengers feeding on dried animal and plant material high in protein, including fur, hair, feathers, and similar materials. Sometimes they are associated with dead animals. Some dermestid beetles adults are found on flowers in the spring and summer, where they feed on pollen.

Larder Beetle *Dermestes lardarius*

The definition of a larder is "a store of food, especially in a home," and this is exactly where you may find a Larder Beetle. It is here that they feed on high-protein dry pet foods, dried grain and dead insects. Wool carpet, old hides, furs and feathers may be on their menu too. They are dark brown with a cream-colored band across the top of its wing covers. It overwinters as an adult and lays eggs in the spring. Larder beetles are most commonly see from May through July.

Soldier Beetles
Family Cantharidae

Appearance
These are small to medium sized beetles, with most species between $1/4$ to $1/2$ inch long. Most species are black or brown, although some are yellowish. They have a somewhat flattened, oval body and the first pair of wings are soft and leathery. Soldier beetles also possess long antennae and long legs. Soldier beetles are similar to fireflies but lack light-producing organs and their heads are visible from above.

Biology
Soldier beetles are commonly found on flowers or foliage where they feed on pollen and nectar during the day. Some species are predaceous, feeding on insects, especially aphids. Soldier beetles are very active and readily fly from plant to plant. Many soldier beetles can protect themselves by secreting defensive chemical compounds to make them distasteful.

Goldenrod Soldier Beetle *Chauliognathus pennsylvanicus*

Check almost any Tansy or Goldenrod from late July until September and you are bound to see a Goldenrod Soldier Beetle or two...or four. It feeds primarily on pollen and can be an important pollinator. It is an active flier Look for the rectangular black spot on the prothorax and an oval black spot on each wing cover. Adults lay eggs at the end of the summer.

Soldier Beetle *Podabrus species*

Possibly a firefly mimic; but unlike fireflies and even other soldier beetles, the front edge of the pronotum is straight and does not cover any portion of the head. Aphids and other soft-bodied insects are the prey of most *Podabrus* soldier beetles. A large genera of over 100 North American species.

Checkered Beetles Family Cleridae

Appearance

Small to moderate very hairy beetles, most between $3/16$ to $1/2$ inch long. They are elongate and cylindrical in shape. The prothorax is narrower than the base of the wing covers while the head is as wide or wider than the pronotum They have moderate length antennae which are often clubbed. Checkered beetles are often brightly colored.

Biology

Checkered beetles are typically found on or under the bark of trees and logs where they are predaceous chiefly on other insects, such as bark beetles. Other species are common on flowers and feed on pollen. A few species are associated with dead animals. Larvae of some species are parasites of solitary bee larvae.

Checkered Beetle *Enoclerus nigripes nigripes*

This colorful checkered beetle is predaceous on borers—especially bark beetles—that are found under of the bark of dying conifer trees. It is reddish with black, white and yellow markings. It is active during the day from spring to early summer.

Red-Blue Checkered Beetle *Trichodes nutalli*

British naturalist Thomas Nutall is a lucky guy to have this beautiful checkered beetle named after him. It is iridescent bluish-green with three vibrant red bands on each wing cover. It is common on flowers in meadows and fields where it feeds on small insects and pollen. Larvae are parasitic on larvae of leafcutter bees. This beetle is active June through August.

Ladybird Beetles
Family Coccinellidae

Appearance

Small, between 1/16 to 3/8 inch long. They are oval and convex beetles with the head mostly hidden underneath the pronotum when viewed from above. They have short, clubbed antennae and relatively short legs. Ladybird beetles typically have a black and white pronotum and have red or orange wing covers with black spots, although they are infrequently black with red or orange spots.

Biology

Ladybird beetles, also commonly called ladybugs, are typically found on leaves, stems, flowers, and other plant parts where they are predaceous on aphids and other soft-bodied insects, although they can supplement their diet with pollen when prey is lacking. A few ladybird beetles are plant feeders. Ladybird beetles overwinter as adults, sometimes in large aggregations. Ladybird beetles can protect themselves against potential enemies by secreting a noxious fluid from leg and body joints, called "reflex bleeding." These beetles can pass through several generations during a year.

Seven-spotted Ladybird *Coccinella septempunctata*

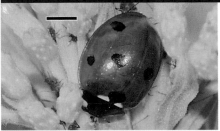

larva

Guess how many spots a Seven-spotted Ladybird Beetle has. Seven black spots on orange wing covers. It's pronotum is black with two white spots. Non-native and likely displacing many native ladybirds! It is found in many types of environments, including fields and gardens where it feeds on aphids. It is active from spring through summer.

Three-banded Ladybird Beetle *Coccinella trifasciata*

The Three-banded Ladybird Beetle is a very northern species that is mostly found north of 40 degrees latitude. It is said to be the most common native *Coccinella* in the Northeast U.S. Found across much of Canada to Alaska. This subspecies is *perplexa*.

Eye-spotted Ladybird Beetle *Anatis mali*

I imagine it is called "eye-spotted" because of the dark pupil-like spots within a lighter ring (the iris?). A lovely ladybird that is reddish brown with 18 black spots ringed in yellow. This ladybird beetle is common on coniferous trees and is active May through July.

Thirteen-spotted Ladybird *Hippodamia tredecimpunctata*

An elongated body shape is typical for *Hippodamia* ladybird beetles. Found across the northern half of the continent. Eighteen species of *Hippodamia* occur north of Mexico, including the next species.

Convergent Ladybird Beetle *Hippodamia convergens*

"Convergent" in two ways; the white stripes on the pronotum are angled as if converging, and in the fall large numbers converge for overwintering. This is the common ladybird beetle sold at gardening centers for controlling aphids in gardens. It is native to North America. May to October.

Spotted Ladybird Beetle *Coleomegilla maculata*

Ten spots on its wing covers and two spots on its pronotum. The pronotum and wing covers are pinkish red. It is found in many types of environments including fields and gardens, but usually in wetlands. It feeds mainly on pollen but also some aphids. It is active from spring through summer.

Spotless Ladybird Beetle *Cycloneda munda*

The Spotless Ladybird Beetle has red to orange wing covers and lacks spots. The pronotum is black with an ornate unique white marking. It is found in a variety of habitats during spring and summer where it feeds on aphids.

Multicolored Asian Ladybird *Harmonia axyridis*

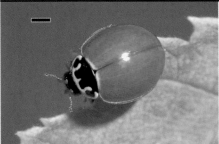

Like its common name implies, this is a non-native species. The Multicolored Asian Ladybird Beetle has reddish to orange wing covers. They often have many spots on the wing covers, variably ranging from none to every multiple of two up to 18. Multicolored Asian Ladybird Beetles are found in many types of environments, including trees and fields where they eat aphids as well as other small soft-bodied insects. They are active from spring into fall and can be a nuisance when over-wintering in homes (photo left).

Two-triangled Ladybird *Anisosticta bitriangularis*

If your feet are wet, you may be in the right place to find this species. Bogs, fens and beaver ponds are just a few of the favorite haunts of this ladybird. "Two-triangled," or *bitriangularis*, likely refers to the grouping of spots on the pronotum.

Ladybird Beetle *Brachiacantha albifrons*

A tiny ladybird beetle spotted with small pale spots. Iridescent eyes. Twenty-five North American *Brachiacantha* species; all are very difficult to identify as their colors and spot patterns are variable within species. Larvae of many *Brachiacantha* species are rarely seen since they feed inside ant nests on scale insects.

Sapfeeding Beetles
Family Nitidulidae

Appearance

Small beetles, most under ¹/₂ inch long. Most have short wing covers leaving part of the abdomen exposed. Most black, some with orange, yellow or red spots.

Biology

Associated with decaying plant matter, such as rotting fruits and vegetables, fungi and oozing sap. Some associated with carrion or flowers.

Picnic Beetle *Glischrochilus fasciatus*

This beetle's ideal picnic involves feasting on rotten fruit, decaying mushrooms and oozing sap. They are active during spring (as early as April) and also during the fall (as late as October). Shiny black with four irregularly shaped orange spots.

Wedge-shaped Beetles
Family Ripiphoridae

Appearance .

Small to moderate sized beetles ranging from ⅛ to ⅗ inch long. They have a humpbacked shape with a blunt, squared off abdomen, giving them a wedge-shaped appearance. The elytra are short and pointed, exposing part of the abdomen. They possess moderately short, fan-like or comb-like antennae. They are black and orange.

Biology

Wedge-shaped beetles are typically found on flowers where they presumably feed on pollen. They also lay eggs there. After hatching, larvae attach themselves to certain types of wasps or bees and carried back to their nests where they are parasitic on the wasp or bee larvae. Adult wedge-shaped beetles are short-lived and are active during August.

Wedge-shaped Beetle *Macrosiagon dimidiata*

This Wedge-shaped Beetle is black with a yellowish orange band across the wing covers. It is common on asters and similar plants. They are active in August.

Flat Bark Beetles
Family Cucujidae

Appearance

Small to medium very flat beetles, up to a little over ½ inch. They are elongate oval and are generally reddish or brownish.

Biology

Found under the loose bark of dead trees and logs. Thought to be predaceous on other insects while some may be fungivorous.

Red Flat Bark Beetle *Cucujus clavipes*

A Red Flat Bark Beetle is red, flat and found under the bark of dead ash and poplar trees. It is good to be flat when navigating such tight spaces. Not only are their eggs laid under bark but the adults also hunt bark beetles and the larva of long-horned beetles there as well.

Tumbling Flower Beetles Family Mordellidae

Appearance

Small insects, generally between ¹/₈ to ¹/₄ inch long. They are humpbacked with the abdomen tapering to point. The head is pointed down and is difficult to see from above. Their bodies are covered with short dense hairs and they are generally black or grayish, uniformly colored, although sometimes with spots.

Look for tumbling flower beetles on umbelliferous flowers where they feed on pollen.

Biology

These beetles are typically associated with umbelliferous flowers (like wild parsley) and composite flowers (like tansy and ox-eye daisy) where they feed on pollen. When they feel threatened they can run quickly or drop and even fly away.

Tumbling Flower Beetle *Hoshihananomia octopunctata*

This tumbling flower beetle species is brownish to grayish black. It has eight yellowish spots or bars on its wing covers and white bands on its abdomen. It is found on flowers during May and July. It has also been reported to be associated with rotting oak logs and dying beech.

Darkling Beetles
Family Tenebrionidae

Appearance

Darkling beetles are usually small to medium beetles, usually between 1/8 to one inch long ranging from elongate oval to oval in shape. They are typically black or brown, although there are few that are brightly marked red. The antennae are moderate in length and are inserted under an brow ridge on the head. Although this is one of the larger groups of beetles in North America, most occur in the west, while relatively few occur in the North Woods.

Biology

Darkling beetles are found under leaf litter, stones, on plants, in rotting wood, associated with fungus, animal nests and dry pet food. Some species are found on sand dunes. Darkling beetles are typically scavengers or fungus feeders. They are usually active at night.

Forked Fungus Beetle *Bolitotherus cornutus*

A Forked Fungus Beetle is robust-bodied and dark brown to black. It is distinctive because of the two prominent horns on the pronotum of males and the warty body. Though maybe not evident from the photo, these beetles are incredibly cryptic. Search for them on hard shelf fungus, its food source, or on old logs from May through August.

Yellow Mealworm *Tenebrio molitor*

A Yellow Mealworm is shiny reddish to dark brown or black. It is associated with dark, quiet areas and is common in bird nests as well as around dead animals. Yellow Mealworms are present during spring and summer.

Roughened Darkling Beetle *Upis ceramboides*

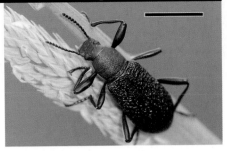

The Roughened Darkling Beetle gets its common name from the textured wing covers. It is elongate and black. It is commonly found under bark but does venture into the light of day. It is active May to August.

Fire-colored Beetles
Family Pyrochroidae

Appearance .
Medium-sized, often black with some red (the "fire" in Fire-colored). Elytra is wider than pronotum and often wider at rear. Head has a distinct neck. Antennae of males often branching.

Biology
Larvae are mostly in decaying wood where they eat fungi. Adult males prod blister beetles into exuding cantharidin, then store the chemical and use it to attract females. Most adults are nocturnal and come to lights on occasion. Also attracted to fermenting fruit and other vegetable matter.

Fire-colored Beetle *Pedilus species*

A brightly colored day-active beetle. Males harass blister beetles until they exude cantharidin, then lick it off their backs, eventually using it to attract females for mating. The cantharidin is transferred to the female in the sperm packet and when her eggs are laid they are coated in the chemical, which protects them until they hatch.

Blister Beetles
Family Meloidae

Appearance

Medium sized insects, usually between ³/₈ to ⁵/₈ inch long. Usually slender bodied with a pronotum narrower than the head or the base of the wing covers. The wing covers are soft and flexible. Usually black or brown, occasionally green. Some are striped and others colorful.

Biology

Most blister beetles are found on plants where they eat leaves and flowers. Some feed on nectar. The bodies of blister beetles contain a chemical known as cantharidin which they secrete to protect themselves. This substance can cause blisters to human skin and can be poisonous if eaten by people or animals. Eggs are laid in the soil or on flowers. Many blister beetles exhibit a rather unusual and complex life cycle known as hypermetamorphosis. The larva is alligator-like when is first hatches. This stage, called a triungulin, is very active. The following stages are grub-like and inactive. Many are associated with bee nests and some feed on grasshopper eggs.

Oil Beetle *Meloe species*

An odd looking beetle that lacks wings but has very short elytra that only cover a portion of the enlarged abdomen. Shiny black with large blue spots on the abdomen. Males significantly smaller than females. If disturbed, they may emit an oil-like substance (cantharidin) from leg joints; hence "oil beetle." Protected by this chemical.

Blister Beetle *Nemognatha lutea lutea*

This blister beetle is reddish with black legs and antennae. Some of the mouthparts are long and slender which it uses to feed on nectar from flowers. It is common June and July.

Gray Blister Beetle *Epicauta fabricii*

Very similar to the Black Blister Beetle (*E. pennsylvanica*) but gray and found in spring and early summer on pea species (*Lathyrus, Vicia*) and lupines (*Lupinus* species). Adults found May through early July (when their food plants are available.

Black Blister Beetle *Epicauta pennsylvanica*

This late summer cousin of the Gray Blister Beetle (*E. fabricii*), feeds mainly on goldenrods (*Solidago* spp.) but also utilizes other herbaceous plants. Note that it is all black and never gray. It is common July through September.

Say's Blister Beetle *Lytta sayi*

An early season beauty that is often found on blossoms of blooming lupines and cherries —hawthorns, juneberries, etc. Found May through early July. Larvae live in bees' nests. This blister beetle has an iridescent dark green head and wing covers with orange and black legs.

Nuttall's Blister Beetle *Lytta nuttalli*

A gorgeous blister beetle of the western Great Plains that just makes it to the western edge of the North Woods in northwestern Minnesota. Too pretty to not include. Adults feed on legumes such as Veiny Pea (*Lathyrus venosus*) and lupines (*Lupinus* species). Larvae feed on the eggs of grasshoppers.

Leaf Beetles
Family Chrysomelidae

Appearance

Generally small beetles, essentially all under ½ inch long. Their shape is variable but are generally oval or elongate oval and convex or flat. They have moderate length antennae. Many leaf beetles are brightly colored and spotted species are easily confused with ladybird beetles. Leaf beetles are the fourth largest group of beetles.

Biology

Leaf beetles are plant feeders feeding primarily on leaves and flowers and are found on nearly all types of plants. Many leaf beetles are particular to specific plants. Adults typically spend the winter as adults.

Sumac Flea Beetle *Blepharida rhois*

A Sumac Flea Beetle has an oval, convex body. It has a reddish brown head and prothorax with cream-colored wing covers with reddish brown markings. It is found on sumac during April through June and again in August and September.

Swamp Milkweed Leaf Beetle *Labidomera clivicollis*

A Swamp Milkweed Leaf Beetle has an oval, convex body. It has an iridescent greenish black head and prothorax and orange wing covers with black spots. It feeds on milkweed during June through July.

Alder Leaf Beetle *Calligrapha alni*

Calligrapha beetles have an oval, convex body. The color is variable but is generally orange with ornate black and/or white markings. They feed on the leaves of a variety of hardwood trees and shrubs. They are common from spring and summer.

Many-spotted Leaf Beetle *Calligrapha multipunctata*

This *Calligrapha* leaf beetle species has an oval, convex body, and is pearl colored with ornate dark markings. It feeds on willow leaves and is common from May to August.

Dogwood Leaf Beetle *Calligrapha rowena*

Calligrapha rowena may be rare in Minnesota and it is certainly spectacular. A beautiful collage of red-orange, black and whitish shapes adorn the wing covers. Feeds on dogwood and the leaves of other shrubs and trees. They are found in spring and summer.

Dogbane Beetle *Chrysochus auratus*

A Dogbane Beetle is oval and convex. It is iridescent green, sometimes with blue and gold. They are common in fields and prairies where they feed on dogbane and milkweed June through August.

Spotted Cucumber Beetle *Diabrotica undecimpunctata*

Also known as the Southern Corn Rootworm as it can be a serious pest on corn (It has made the "Top 10 Worst Insect Pests" lists of several organizations.) But you will not only find it on corn and cucumbers as it has been recorded on more than 200 species of plants. Active late June through August.

Bean Leaf Beetle *Cerotoma trifurcata*

Orange beetle with a checkerboard of four black spots on its wing covers; but can be red or yellow and can lack the spots. Sometimes a pest on crops. There has been a documented infestation of a commercial pumpkin field in Minnesota. But, as its common name implies, it can be a serious pest to beans.

Elm Leaf Beetle *Xanthogaleruca luteola*

Elm leaves is where you might find either the adults or the larvae of this leaf beetle. The larvae skeletonize the undersides of leaves while adults chew small holes in the leaves. Severe defoliation may weaken the elm and make it more susceptible to diseases. Active May to June and again August to September.

Cottonwood Leaf Beetle *Chrysomela scripta*

A Cottonwood Leaf Beetle is ¼ inch long with an oval, convex body. It has a black head, a red and black prothorax, and yellowish wing covers with black markings. A cottonwood leaf beetle feeds on cottonwood and poplar leaves throughout spring and summer.

Colorado Potato Beetle *Leptinotarsa decemlineata*

Native to Mexico and originally fed on nightshade (*Solonum*), but spread throughout North America with cultivated potatoes where it's a crop pest. Note their ten black stripes that separates them from similar species.

Striped Willow Leaf Beetle *Disonycha alternata*

Like most *Disonycha* leaf beetle species, this one is small and colorful. Most feed on "weeds" and not valuable crops; this species feeds on willows. If you look closely at this photo you can see the notched corners of the pronotum. This is characteristic of *Disonycha* species. Widespread in North America.

Flea Beetle *Disonycha pensylvanica*

Enlarged back legs enable this leaf beetle to jump (This how it got its common name). It has a reddish orange and black prothorax with two black spots and black and yellow striped wing covers. It feeds on knotweeds (*Polygonum* spp.) and is common May to July.

Casebearing Leaf Beetle *Pachybrachis species*

Tiny leaf beetles with a distinct shape. More than 150 species in North America. Variable in color and pattern, even within species, and, as a result, difficult to identify.

Long-horned Leaf Beetle   *Plateumaris species*

Like the two species below, this leaf beetle is intimately tied to aquatic plants. The larval host plants of this genus include Sweet Flag (*Acorus*), sedges (*Carex*), bulrushes (*Scirpus*), rushes (*Juncus*) and Marsh Marigold (*Caltha palustris*). Very common around a Beaver-dammed pond in June.

Water-lily Leaf Beetle   *Donacia species*

Watch for these iridescent gold or bronze beetles on floating leaves as you paddle your canoe. They have relatively long antennae for a leaf beetle, about half the length of body, with wing covers with a series of small pits. They are found on aquatic plants, like water lilies, where they feed on pollen from June to August.

Water-lily Beetle   *Galerucella nymphaeae*

Though its Latin name indicates a preference for white water-lilies (*Nymphaea* species), it actually prefers Bullhead Lily (*Nuphar luteum*) and Water Shield (*Brasenia schreberi*). Eggs are laid on top of the floating leaves, which the developing larvae devour. They can't swim so they must float to the next leaf to continue development.

Tenspotted Leaf Beetle   *Xanthonia decemnotata*

A tiny but stout leaf beetle. It is reddish brown with ten small black spots on its wing covers. It is found in wooded areas associated with oak and can be found in July.

Goldenrod Leafminer *Microrphopala vittata*

Goldenrod Leafminer has a red head and prothorax. The wing covers are blue black and red with a series of small punctures. Larvae mine between the layers of goldenrod leaves (and other hosts) leaving curving, discolored trails in their wake. May through August.

Leaf Beetle *Ophraella conferta*

This drab but distinctively striped leaf beetle feeds on goldenrod (*Solidago* spp.) leaves (as in this photo). This photo was taken in mid July.

Milkweed Tortoise Beetle *Chelymorpha cassidea*

A Milkweed Tortoise Beetle is oval and convex. It is orange with six black spots on the pronotum and six black spots on each wing cover. The head is hidden underneath the pronotum. It is found in fields during spring and summer where it feeds on morning glory and occasionally milkweed.

Sunflower Tortoise Beetle *Physonota helianthi*

One of two eastern *Physonota* tortoise beetles; *P. unipunctata* is not green and feeds on bergamots (bee balms) (*Monarda* spp.) and the one pictured here feeds on sunflowers (*Helianthus* spp.). Note that the specific epithet *helianthi* refers to this feeding preference.

Family *Chrysomelidae* LEAF BEETLES | **123**

Long-horned Beetles
Family Cerambycidae

Appearance

Small to large insects, ranging in size from 1/8 up to almost 2 1/2 inches long. They are elongate, some are almost triangular, and cylindrical. They have long antennae, at least half the length of the body with many species possessing antennae as long as the body or longer. The antennae are typically at least partly surround by the compound eyes. They vary widely in color ranging from black, brown, grayish, red, yellow, and/or orange.

Biology

Most long-horned beetles are wood borers attacking dying or recently dead trees. Some species are stem borers. Adults are commonly found trees and under loose bark. Many are also found on flowers. Long-horned beetles may feed on leaves, pollen or wood. Longhorn beetles typically spend the winter as larvae, maturing into adults in the spring.

Northeastern Sawyer *Monochamus notatus*

The Northeaster Sawyer has antennae longer than its body. The pronotum is mottled with light and dark patches and a conspicuous spine. It is grayish brown with small light and dark spots on the wing covers. Sawyers are associated with dying spruce and balsam fir and adults are found from June through August.

White-spotted Sawyer *Monochamus scutellatus*

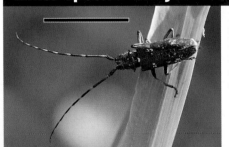

Have you ever heard a creaking rocking chair at night in the North Woods? That is the roundheaded wood borer larva chewing its way through down and dead fir and pine logs.

Long-horned Beetle *Microgoes oculatus*

"*Oculatus*" —the Latin specific epithet of this attractive species —presumably refers to the two black eyespots on the elytra. Like other long-horned beetles it can be found under, and on, the bark of a variety of trees and shrubs. This one was on an Eastern White Pine.

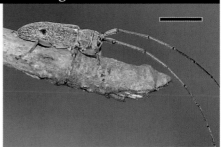

Red Milkweed Beetle *Tetraopes tetrophthalmus*

Look no further than the local patch of Common Milkweed (*Asclepias syriaca*) for this striking longhorn. Eggs are laid near milkweed plants in grass stems. The larva find their way to the milkweed plant and burrow into the roots where they develop. They feed on milkweed and are commonly found when milkweed plants are around.

Red-femured Milkweed Borer *Tetraopes femoratus*

Normally associated with Showy Milkweed (*Asclepias speciosa*) in the west, they are sometimes found on Common Milkweed in the North Woods. Though similar to *T. tetrophthalmus*, note the contrasting black and white antenna banding and smaller scutellum spots. Both beetles have divided eyes; the antenna arising between.

Raspberry Cane Borer *Oberea bimaculata*

A Raspberry Cane Borer has a black head and antennae. The prothorax is reddish brown with two black spots while the wing covers are bluish gray. This long-horned borer lays eggs in raspberries and blackberries (*Rubus* spp.) and is found from May to July.

Locust Borer   *Megacyllene robiniae*

The resemblance to wasps may deter some predators. Black with thin yellow markings, the second band on the wing covers **W**-shaped. Eggs laid in living Black Locust (*Robinia pseudoacacia*), a tree not native to the North Woods, but used in ornamental plantings. Found on flowers, especially on goldenrod (*Solidago* spp.) in August and September.

Long-horned Beetle   *Clytus ruricola*

Clytus long-horned beetles are mainly North Woods species. They develop in the rotting trunks of maples. Like the Locust Borer, this long-horned beetle is a wasp mimic and often found on flowers. It has relatively short antennae for an long-horned beetle. Distinctive yellow markings. Active June through August.

Elderberry Borer   *Desmocerus palliatus*

Elderberry shrubs (*Sambucus* spp.) are the host for the larva of this magnificent beetle. Eggs are laid in the stems of elderberry. When the larva hatch, they bore down through the stem to the roots. It takes a full two years for the life cycle to be completed. Variable as adults; Blue areas may appear black and orange area may be yellow. May through July.

Long-horned Beetle   *Evodinus monticola*

The bark of coniferous trees is where you might find this attractive long-horned beetle; but like its cousins in the subfamily lepturinae, it often feeds on flowers. Also note on this species and the following flower long-horns that the pronotum is bell-shaped and the elytra tapers at the rear. Northern U.S. and Canada.

Long-horned Beetle *Judolia montivagans*

A member of the subfamily Lepturinae or the "flower long-horns;" Members (*Desmocerus, Evodinus, Judolia, Leptura, Stictoleptura, Typocerus* species) feast on the pollen of blooming flowers. Lays its eggs in dying evergreens (pine and spruce) as well some hardwoods (poplar and willow). June through August.

Long-horned Beetle *Leptura plebeja*

Another of the "flower long-horns" that feeds on pollen of blooming flowers. Queen Anne's Lace (*Daucos carota*) is a favorite species. *Leptura* larvae develop inside rotting, usually moist wood and often show little preference for a specific tree species.

Long-horned Beetle *Leptura subhamata*

This boldly marked longhorn's larva develop inside dead pine and hemlock (a tree only found in the eastern portions of the North Woods). It has a yellow-ish tan body with a black cross across its wing covers. Common July and August.

Red-shouldered Pine Borer *Stictoleptura canadensis*

Some Red-shouldered Pine Borers have not only red "shoulders," but completely red wing covers. Banded antennae help distinguish this species from similar longhorns.

Family *Cerambycidae* LONG-HORNED BEETLES **127**

Long-horned Beetle *Strangalepta abbreviata*

Strangalepta abbreviata is a beautiful longhorn, glossy black with an orange longitudinal band on each wing cover. This longhorn beetle is associated with dying spruce and is common on flowers and foliage from June to August.

Long-horned Beetle *Strangalia acuminata*

Many specimens of *Strangalepta acuminata* show much more yellow on the elytra (wing covers) than this one, and they can even be orange or red. Note the orange femurs and the all black pronotum, head and antennae. This is likely a male as the abdomen extends beyond the elytra.

Long-horned Beetle *Typocerus velutinus velutinus*

This flower long-horned beetle has a dark-colored head, prothorax, and antennae while the wing covers are reddish brown with four yellow bands or pairs of spots. The legs are yellow, reddish brown and dark brown. Associated with a variety of dying trees. Adults are common at flowers in July and August.

Long-horned Beetle *Cosmosalia chrysocoma*

A densely fuzzy species covered in golden hairs. Larvae feed on decaying wood of hardwood and coniferous trees. Adults feed on pollen. June to September.

Weevils & Bark Beetles Family Curculionidae

Appearance

Small to medium size beetles that are generally elongate oval and cylindrical. Weevils are conspicuous as the head is prolonged into a snout or beak. This snout can be relatively short and blunt or can be slender and long (sometimes longer than the entire body length of the weevil). They have short, elbowed antennae. Many species are drab colored with some resembling bark. Some species are brightly colored. Weevils are the second largest family of beetles.

Biology

Weevils are plant feeders, feeding on a wide variety of plants, attacking leaves, trunks, branches, stems, fruits, seeds, and roots. Some species have a wide host range while others have a much narrower list of preferred plants. Many weevils will play dead when they feel threatened.

Weevil *Lepyrus palustris*

A large weevil; brown with a moderate length snout. It is associated with willow and other marsh vegetation. It is found in July and August.

Weevil *Lixus caudifer*

Like *Lepyrus palustris* (above), this large and attractive weevil is associated with marsh vegetation. This specimen was photographed on willow near a beaver pond in late June. Note the divergent wing cover tips (like tiny "tails") and the broad pronotum that merges smoothly with the wing covers.

Weevil *Listronotus delumbis*

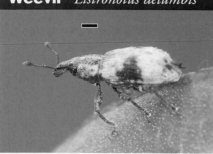

A pale weevil with dark triangles on its elytra. Usually found in wetlands and often on Broad-leaved Arrowhead (*Sagittaria latifolia*). This specimen was photographed on this species when it was blooming in a small pond in mid July). June to August.

Weevil *Mononychus vulpeculus*

Photographed on its home turf—Wild Iris (*Iris versicolor*); This weevil is associated with irises where it lays its eggs in the seeds. It has a short snout which is deflexed down. It has a brown head and beak while the upper surface of the prothroax and the wing covers are grayish black. The sides of the protho-rax are brown as are the legs. The sides of the abdomen are white. It is found mostly in May and June—when Irises are blooming—although it can also be seen later in the summer.

Green Immigrant Leaf Weevil *Polydrusus sericeus*

Maybe you've seen these little green guys on your own shoul-der, arm or leg in mid summer; they seem to hitchhike on humans. They have a short broad snout and are covered with metallic green scales. It feeds on the leaves of many dif-ferent shrubs and hardwood trees; especially Yellow Birch. Its common name may tip off the fact that this little weevil is an immigrant from Europe, first recorded in North America from New York in the early 1900s. This weevil is found spring and summer.

Weevil *Smicronyx constrictus*

This weevil has a long slender beak which is nearly as long as its body. It is reddish brown with light colored scales on the legs and underside. It is generally associated with herbaceous plants in the aster family where eggs are laid into the seeds. They are active during July and August.

Weevil *Tychius species*

This weevil is only $1/16$ inch long including a moderate length snout. They are dark colored covered with whitish scales. They are associated with legumes (pea family: Fabaceae) where eggs are typically laid in seeds. This weevil is found in July and August

Warren Root Collar Weevil *Hylobius warreni*

Adults may live for five years! They overwinter at the base of a conifer. Jack Pine, Red Pine and White Spruce are the victims of the larvae which feed under the bark at root collar level. Their bored galleries cause the tree to ooze pitch resin. If they encircle the trunk with their borings the tree may be susceptible to wind damage.

Nut Weevil *Curculio nasicus*

This Nut Weevil has a long slender snout that is about as long as its body. Females have a longer rostrum than males. It is an olive, brownish color with a light colored underside. Nut weevils use their beak to bore into nuts in order to lay eggs. Watch for nut weevils in July.

Alderflies, Dobsonflies & Lacewings
Order Neuroptera

Diversity
There are 15 families and 401 species in North America. Nerve-winged insects are fairly common in the North Woods.

Appearance
Adults: Nerve-winged insects are small to large, ranging from $1/8$ to two inches long. They have elongate, cylindrical, soft-bodies with a long, slender abdomen and well-developed legs. They have chewing mouthparts and long, slender antennae that are occasionally is clubbed. They have four, similarly sized membranous wings that are usually longer than the abdomen with a characteristic net-like arrangement of veins. These wings are held over their body, typically tent-like when at rest. Nerve-winged insects are not very strong flyers.

Larvae: Nerve-winged larvae are typically cylindrical or some what flattened with a conspicuous head. They possess either chewing or sickle-like sucking mouthparts which face forward. Nerve-winged larvae have conspicuous legs and lack prolegs. The abdomen of aquatic species possesses filaments sticking out to the side.

Habitats
Nerve-winged insects are common in a variety of terrestrial sites, such as deciduous or conifer forests and nearby areas and sites adjacent to rivers, lakes, ponds and other water. The larvae are either terrestrial in the same sites or are aquatic.

Life Cycle
Nerve-winged insects are holometabolous insects, using complete metamorphosis to develop.

Food
Adult nerve-winged insects are usually predacious on aphids and other insects or feed on nectar and pollen. Some adults are short-lived and do not feed. The larvae are nearly always predacious on other insects. Eggs are generally laid in the soil, on the tips of stalks on plants, or objects near water. Look for nerve-winged insects May to September.

Don't confuse them with...

...dragonflies and damselflies. You can distinguish between them as dragonflies and damselflies have very short, straight antennae (never clubbed). Stoneflies also look similar but are more flattened and possess legs that are more widely spaced out. Sometimes caddisflies are confused but they have hairy wings and very long antennae (as long or longer than their bodies). Mantids (not native to the North Woods) could be confused with certain nerve-winged insects but mantids have leathery wings and longer antennae.

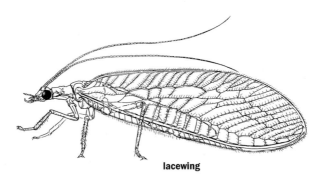

lacewing

Alderflies
Family Sialidae

Appearance

Alderflies have a 3/16 to 1/4 inch long black body with a smoky wings; the hind wings are broad at the base.

Biology

Eggs are laid on emergent vegetation along slow moving streams and lakes. The larvae are aquatic insect predators. They pupate on shore in soil or wet plant litter. Alderflies are found on foliage and other nearby objects close to water, although they are attracted to lights and can be further away. They are present May and June.

Alderfly *Sialis velata*

Females often guard their eggs by perching vertically to aquatic plant stems, their eggs underneath them attached to the stem.

Dobsonflies & Fishflies
Family Corydalidae

Appearance

These are often large insects ranging in size up to 1/2 to two inches long. They have large mandibles and have hind wings that are broad at the base. They are typically brown.

Biology

Dobsonflies and fishflies lay eggs on branches hanging over streams or lakes. Once the larvae hatch they drop into the water. Eventually they pupate on the shore in soil or wet plant litter. Adults are found on foliage and stones near streams and lakes, although they are attracted to lights and can range away from water. They are active from May to August.

Dobsonfly *Corydalus cornutus*

Disturbingly large mandibles; in fact, males have mandibles up to 3/4 inch long which they use for fighting other male dobsonflies. Despite its appearance, a male cannot bite people, although it is possible that the female could bite if handled carelessly. A Dobsonfly is 1 1/2 to 2 inches long and brown with smoky wings that have tiny white spots on the forewings. Dobsonflies are associated with streams and are common July and August.

Spring Fishfly *Chauliodes rastricornis*

Your first encounter with this species will likely be along a lakeshore or river bank in early summer. They are active May to July. A fishfly is large—1/2 to 1 inch long—and gray brown with smoky wings. They have saw-like or comb-like antennae.

Dark Fishfly *Nigronia serricornis*

Nigronia fasciata

Distinctively marked, Dark Fishflies are creatures of clean small streams, often trout streams with riffles and rapids. They have blackish wings with white blotches. *Nigronia fasciata* (right image) has more white (forming a band) than *N. serricornis* (left image) whose white is limited to a small triangle. Note the saw-like or comb-like antennae. Their fluttering, slow flight is moth-like but their long abdomen hangs down. Common June and July.

Mantidflies
Family Mantisipidae

Appearance

Mantidflies are 3/8 to 5/8 inch long. They have a prolonged prothorax, the area directly behind the head, and have large front legs modified for grabbing prey. Mantidflies are reddish brown or dark brown; wings are either partly brown or are entirely clear.

Biology

As larvae, Mantidflies parasitize the egg sacs of spiders or live in the soil where the larvae prey on scarab beetle grubs, noctuid moth larvae, or social wasps. The larvae go through a type of development known as hypermetamorphosis where the first instar (stage) of the larva is very active and the subsequent instars become grub-like. Mantidfly adults prey on small insects they capture. They are active during June and September.

The raptorial front legs of the Brown Mantidfly are used to capture and hold insect prey.

Brown Mantidfly *Climaciella brunnea*

At first glance this insect looks remarkably like a *Polistes* paper wasp. But a closer look will reveal long, mantid-like folded front legs and a distinctive and very non-wasplike head. Reddish brown body with yellow markings. Its wings are brownish along the front margin with the rest being clear. This mantidfly parasitizes wolf spider eggs. After hatching the larvae attach themselves to the back of the adult spider to feed and wait for an opportunity to penetrate a freshly formed egg case to feed on the eggs. Adults are common on foliage and flowers in wooded areas. Look for them June to September.

Brown Lacewings
Family Hemerobiidae

Appearance

Brown lacewings are 1/8 to 1/4 inch long. They have a brown body with somewhat smoky wings and brown veins.

Biology

Brown lacewings prefer to live in wooded areas where they lay their eggs on plants. They feed on soft-bodied insects, including aphids; they will also feed on pollen and scavenge on dead insects. The larvae—known as "aphid wolves"—are predacious on aphids. Brown lacewings usually spend the winter as pupae, although they can overwinter as adults. Brown lacewings are present May to September (or later). Look for adults at lights at night.

Brown Lacewing *Hemerobius species*

Hemerobius brown lacewings sometimes spend the winter as adults. Therefore, look for this brown lacewing early in the spring and late in the fall—from May to September (or later). This group of brown lacewings have somewhat more oval wings compared to others. Otherwise you need to examine the slight differences in the pattern of the veins.

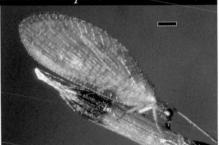

Green Lacewings
Family Chrysopidae

Appearance

Green lacewings are 3/8 to 7/16 inch long. They are generally greenish with coppery colored eyes and have clear wings with greenish veins.

eggs

Biology

Green lacewings are found on herbaceous plants as well as trees and shrubs. They are predacious on soft-bodied insects, especially aphids, or they feed on pollen or honeydew. They attach their eggs on stalks anchored to plants. The larvae—known as "aphid lions"— are predacious on aphids and similar soft-bodied insects; some larvae may cover themselves with debris to better ambush pre and avoid detection by ants, the chief protectors of aphids. Eventually they pupate on the underside of leaves. Green lacewings are active at dusk or a night and are often attracted to lights. They are present May to September.

larva

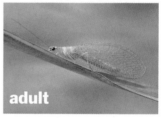
adult

Green Lacewing *Chrysopa chi*

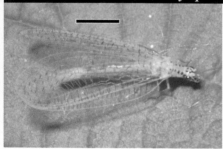

Be careful not to disturb this guy! This green lacewing and similar species can produce a bad smell if disturbed. Often first noticed by their weak fluttering flight. Stunning golden eyes. They are bluish green with black spots on the head and prothorax. Venation of wing separates genus *Chrysopa* from similar genus *Chrysoperla*. This species has an X-shaped mark between the antennal bases, two spots on top of head and three pairs of dark spots on the pronotum. The adults are predacious on aphids. Common spring and summer.

Antlions
Family Myrmeleontidae

Appearance

Antlions are one to $1^1/2$ inches long. Their abdomen is long and slender, often longer than the wings, resembling a damselfly. The antennae are not quite as long compared to other nerve-winged insects and are clubbed. They are brownish and have wings that are clear or with dark color spots.

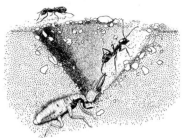

Larvae lie in wait buried in soil, or make pits in dry dusty soil in protected areas. They actually flip sand or dirt on to potential victims to cause them to slide down.

Biology

Adults apparently are scavengers on plant and animal material or are predacious. They deposit eggs into soil especially sandy ones. Larvae (also known as "doodlebugs") are predacious and either hunt prey or construct conical pits (illustration right) and wait concealed at the bottom for prey to fall in. They overwinter as larvae in the soil. Adults are active at dusk and night and some are attracted to lights. They are present June to August.

Many folks know antlion larva as "doodle-bugs." Top photo is the typical waiting position. Bottom photo is of a larva removed from its pit.

Antlion   *Brachynemurus nebulosus*

Large attractive insects that are named for their larval stage; "Antlion" refers to the diet and predatory nature of the larva. Adults wings have a series of dark brown spots as well as a white spot near the tip of each forewing. Antlion adults are active June to August.

Sawflies, Wasps, Bees & Ants
Order Hymenoptera

Diversity
There are 74 families and about 20,000 species in North America, making this group one of the largest insect orders. The sawflies, wasps, bees, and ants are very common in the North Woods.

Appearance
Adults: Sawflies, wasps, bees, and ants are generally cylindrical-shaped insects that range from slender to robust. Sawflies and horntails have the abdomen broadly joined to the body, while all other Hymenoptera have a narrowed or waist-like attachment to the body. They possess conspicuous mandibles. Their antennae are variable in form but are generally slender, ranging from short to very long. They have four membranous wings which varies from few to a moderate number of veins. The first pair of wings are longer than the hind wings and sometimes held straight over their body. Some species lack wings. The females of many species have conspicuous ovipositors while others possess short, sting-like ovipositors. The remaining ants, wasps, and bees usually have stingers which are modified ovipositors.

Larvae: Sawfly larvae are caterpillar-like possessing a conspicuous head and mandibles. They also have conspicuous true legs and six to ten prolegs on the abdomen. Other Hymenoptera larvae are grub-like with an inconspicuous head and lacking legs.

Habitats
Hymenoptera are found in essentially all terrestrial habitats in the North Woods. They particularly seek out warmth and are found in woodlands, forest edges, fields, and prairies where they are found on foliage, flowers, on trunks and branches, and in the ground.

Life Cycle
Sawflies, wasps, bees, and ants are holometabolous insects, using complete metamorphosis to develop. They typically produce one generation during the year. In the Hymenoptera, fertilized eggs develop into females while males are produced from unfertilized eggs. Certain bees

Cutaway view of a Bald-faced Hornet nest

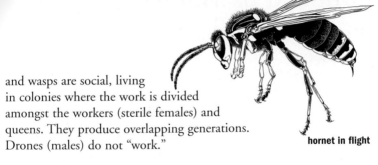

hornet in flight

and wasps are social, living in colonies where the work is divided amongst the workers (sterile females) and queens. They produce overlapping generations. Drones (males) do not "work."

Food

Adult Hymenoptera generally feed on nectar, honeydew, and plant secretions. Sawfly larvae are plant feeders, feeding on leaves, needles and boring into trees. Many wasps are parasitic on other insects, i.e. they lay eggs on or in prey which the hatching larvae slowly consuming after they hatch, eventually killing the host. The larvae of social and solitary wasps eat paralyzed insects or spiders which are provided to them. Bee larvae are provided nectar and pollen.

Don't confuse them with...

...lacewings and other nerve-winged insects. You can distinguish between them as nerve-winged insects have more numerous and complex net-like system of veins in the wings, both pairs of wings are similar in size and held roof-like over their bodies. Some Hymenoptera may also be confused with Diptera. However the true flies have only two wings and sucking mouthparts, and usually inconspicuously small antennae. Some moths are similar to some Hymenoptera. However moths have scales on at least part of the wings and have long, slender, coiling, sucking mouthparts.

Cimbicid Sawflies
Family Cimbicidae

Appearance

Moderate to large sized, stout insects, typically measuring ⁵/₁₆ to one inch in size characterized by moderate-length clubbed antennae. Cimbicid sawflies are usually dark-colored, although some species have reddish abdomens.

Biology

Cimbicid sawflies lay their eggs on a variety of hardwood trees where the larvae feed on the leaves. They are generally active June and July.

Elm Sawflies do resemble large flies.

Elm Sawfly *Cimbex americana*

sawfly larva

Easily mistaken for a huge fly, the Elm Sawfly has smoky colored wings, orange clubbed antennae and a small white spot on the anterior section of the abdomen. The abdomen can be rusty red in males and striped black and cream in females. Though called the "Elm" Sawfly, (elms are not common in the North Woods) this species will also lays eggs on willow, poplar, maple, basswood and alder, where the caterpillar-like larvae feed on leaves during summer.

Horntails
Family Siricidae

Appearance

Large, thick-bodied insects, measuring from 3/4 to 1 3/8 inch long. They get their name from a hornlike plate on the upper tip of the abdomen which on males is relatively short while it is longer and somewhat spearlike in females. Females also possess a conspicuous ovipositor. Horntails are generally dark-colored metallic blue, black, or brown with red or yellow on their legs and abdomens.

Biology

Horntails are usually associated with conifer trees, although at least one species attacks hardwood trees. They lay eggs into trees that have either recently died or are in a greatly weakened condition. The larvae are parasitized by *Megarhyssa* wasps. They are typically found July to September.

Pigeon Tremex (Pigeon Horntail) *Tremex columba*

Huge and distinctive. A Pigeon Tremex is reddish brown with long, amber-colored wings. The photo is of a female; Her stiff ovipositor is used to lay eggs in maple trees (also oak, elm, hickory, apple and birch). She injects the tree with a wood-rotting fungus to allow the larva to more easily bore. Adults are most active during August and September.

Common Sawflies
Family Tenthredinidae

Appearance

They are small to medium insects, generally slender to medium bodied, usually from 3/16 to 3/4 inch long. Their thorax is broadly joined to the abdomen and they usually have short, slender antennae. Common sawflies are dark-colored insects, some species with bright colors, white, yellow, orange, patches or bands on the legs or body.

Biology

Common sawflies are common on foliage and sometimes on flowers. They lay eggs on various trees and

Sawfly larvae resemble caterpillars. These are *Nematus* larvae.

shrubs where the larvae often feed on externally on the leaves or needles, although a few are leafminers, stem borers, or gall formers. They typically overwinter as pupae in the ground or in cocoons in exposed areas. Common sawflies are found throughout the spring and summer.

Common Sawfly   *Dolerus apricus*

This common sawfly is about 3/16 inch long and is black with an orange abdomen with a black tip. Adults are active May to July.

Common Sawfly   *Nematus species*

This common sawfly is slender to stout-bodied. Females are commonly reddish brown while males are black. The group of sawflies is associated with hardwood trees and shrubs and is found spring and summer.

Pear Sawfly *Caliroa cerasi*

Introduced around the world, the Pear Sawfly is likely native to Europe. It is mostly dark-colored. It lays eggs on a variety of hardwood trees and shrubs including cherry and pear, hawthorn and juneberry where slug-like larvae ("Pear Slug") feed on one layer of the leaves. Adults are active spring and summer.

Common Sawfly *Paracharactus rudis*

This sawfly is about 1/8 inch long. It has a black body with an orange thorax. It is associated with grasses and sedges. Adults are found in July and August.

Common Sawfly *Tenthredo species*

A very convincing mimic of ichneumon wasps, this group of common sawflies are slender-bodied, large-headed and often brightly colored with yellow or orange on their legs and bodies. *Tenthredo* sawflies are unusual because they are predaceous. Watch for them spring and summer.

Ichneumon Wasps
Family Ichneumonidae

Appearance

Antennae usually as long or longer than the body. The ovipositors of some are longer than the body, and cannot be withdrawn into the body. Diverse in size and color. This is one of the largest groups of all insects.

Biology

Ichneumonid wasps are solitary wasps that are parasitic on other insects: larvae and pupae of butterflies and moths, flies, sawflies, beetles, lacewings and caddisflies, as well as spiders, scorpionflies, and even other Hymenoptera. Sometimes an individual species attacks a wide variety of hosts, while others are quite specific. Some ichneumonid wasps are hyperparasitic, that is they attack other wasp and fly parasitoids (parasites). Most ichneumonids are endoparastic, i.e. feeding inside the body of their host. Those parastizing wood boring hosts are ectoparasitic, i.e. feeding on the outside of the body. Ichneumonid wasps are seen during spring and summer on flowers and foliage.

Giant Ichneumon   *Megarhyssa macrurus*

One of the "mega" ichneumons. This female has been caught in the act of ovipositing an egg into the larva of another wasp, the Pigeon Horntail (see page 143). Foresters often call these wasps "stump stabbers."

Giant Ichneumon   *Megarhyssa atrata*

Giant Ichneumons are 1 to 1¹/₂ inches long with an ovipositor that can be as long as three inches long. They are black with an orange-yellow head and legs. Giant Ichneumons attack horntails that are boring in hardwood trees. They are common from May until July.

Ichneumon Wasp *possibly Rhyssa species*

This large ichneumon was actively searching a pile of old logs for a host in which to lay its eggs. The ovipositor on this female is as long as the wasp's body. Photo taken in early July.

Ichneumon Wasp *Thyreodon atricolor*

Day-active and huge, this *Thyreodon* wasp is not easily overlooked. The yellow antennae and trailing yellow hind legs are easily visible in this slow-flying species. It searches for the fat caterpillars of sphinx moths in which to lay its eggs.

Ichneumon Wasp *Mesostenine species*

Though seemingly distinctively colored, most ichneumon wasps cannot be identified (even to genus) by photographs.

Ichneumon Wasp *Ichneumon clasma*

This ichneumonid wasp has a black head and thorax with yellow markings. The male abdomen is black with yellow bands. It has mostly yellow legs with some black. This ichneumonid wasp parasitizes certain moth pupae and has a very short ovipositor. Look for them from June into September.

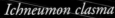

Ichneumon Wasp   *Exacaverus species*

This ichneumonid wasp has black with white on its head and thorax. It's abdomen is black with bluish bands with legs that are white, orange, and some blue (most other species in this genus are dark brown with narrow yellowish bands on the abdomen.). It parasitizes sawflies and is found May to July.

Ichneumon Wasp   *Ophion nigrovarius*

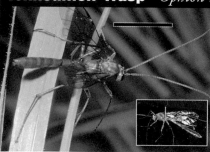

This *Ophion* is reddish brown with some yellowish markings on the head and abdomen which is strongly flattened. Females have relatively short ovipositors. Although most *Ophion* species parasitize noctuid moths, this species attacks June beetles (*Phyllophaga* spp.). May and June. Many similar reddish species in several genera come to lights (inset).

Ichneumon Wasp   *Theronia species*

This ichneumonid wasp species has a black head and a shiny reddish brown thorax and abdomen and dark colored wings. It parasitizes caterpillars of tiger moths and notodontid moths. It is common June and July.

Ichneumon Wasp   *Agrothereutes abbreviator iridescens*

This ichneumonid has a black head and thorax and reddish and black abdomen and legs. This ichneumonid parasitizes sawflies and is found from June through September.

Ichneumon Wasp *Pycnocryptus director*

This ichneumonid wasp has a black head and thorax and reddish and black legs. Its abdomen is mostly red with some black and a white band at the tip of the abdomen and a white band on the antenna. Although this is a common species, it hosts are not known. May to August.

Pelecinid Wasp
Family Pelecinidae

Appearance

There is only one species of this family in North America. The female is very large, measuring about two to three inches long with a very long, slender abdomen. The rarely seen male is about half as long as the female with a shorter club-like abdomen. Both are black with moderately long antennae.

Biology

A pelecinid wasp is a parasite of June beetle white grubs found in the soil. It uses its long abdomen to probe into the soil until it reaches the larvae to lay its eggs. They also appear to parasitize other insect larvae found in rotted wood. Despite its fearsome size and long abdomen, it does not possess a stinger and is harmless to people. It is active from July to September.

Pelecinid Wasp *Pelecinus polyturator*

♀

An insect of late summer and early fall sure to attract attention due to its impressive abdomen length. This is a female who may be searching for June beetle grubs (*Phyllophaga* spp.) to lay her eggs in. Her larvae will develop inside the beetle grubs. As one naturalist noted; She has "swollen ankles" on her hind legs.

body length

Leaf-cutting Bees
Family Megachilidae

Appearance

Moderate sized, stout bodied, wide-headed, hairy insects, ¼ to ¾ inches long. Generally dark-colored, sometimes metallic blue and occasionally with striped abdomens. Unlike other bees, leaf-cutting bees collect pollen on the underside of the abdomen. Long tongues.

Biology

Leaf-cutting bees are solitary insects that live in nests they line with pieces of leaves they cut. Nests are in natural cavities they find in wood or in the ground. They provision the nest with pollen that is carried under their abdomen. Look for them on foliage or flowers in spring and summer.

A leaf-cutting bee emerges from its ground nest. Some nest in wood.

A cut-away view of the leaf-lined nest of a leaf-cutter bee. Larva will develop inside individual cells.

Note the pollen-collecting hairs under the abdomen.

Leaf-cutting Bee   *Megachile species*

Pollen is collected on special hairs under the abdomen. The bright yellow pollen can be seen on the bee even in flight. Like their name suggests, leaf-cutting bees cut circular-shaped holes in the leaves of roses (Wild Rose pictured) and other plants in which to line their nests. Nests may be in natural cavities or often in manmade structures such as rotting wood in old decks, flower boxes, etc. One documented case found 1000 pieces of leaves lining the cells of a nest. Watch for leaf-cutting bees spring and summer.

Halictid Bees (Sweat Bees) Family Halictidae

Appearance

Small to moderate, 1/8 to 3/8 inches long, fuzzy insects. They are commonly metallic green or blue or black or brown often whitish abdominal bands. Their back legs are flattened and hairy to carry pollen. They have short tongues for drinking nectar.

Biology

Solitary insects that nest in clay and sandy stream banks, and even in bare patches in lawns. Although they nest singly, they can form gregarious congregations. They get their name because some species are attracted to the perspiration of people. Common on flowers during spring and summer.

Sweat Bee *Lasioglossum species*

A true sweat bee, *Lasioglossum* species will land on your sweaty arm or leg. A muted iridescent green.

Splendid Metallic Green Bee *Agapostemon splendens*

Splendid is right! Vivid iridescent green head and thorax transitions to a striped yellow and black abdomen in males and an iridescent green abdomen in females. Fine punctures over its body. Note the pollen attached to the hind legs. It is found in spring and summer. Can be common on sandy beaches and dune habitats.

♂

♀

Honey Bees & Bumble Bees, etc. Family Apidae

Appearance

These common bees vary in size from ¼ to one inch long. They are black and brown, black and yellow, or dark bluish green. They have back legs modified for carrying pollen and have long tongues for obtaining nectar.

Biology

Honey bees and bumble bees are social insects, establishing colonies while carpenter bees and digger bees are solitary bees. They are common around flowers spring and summer.

Honey Bee *Apis melifera*

Economically a very important player in American agriculture. But they are believed to be aliens brought to Jamestown in 1621-22. A Honey Bee is social, typically living in human-made hives, although wild honey bee colonies can occur in hollow trees. They construct their nest through a series of vertical hexagonally shaped wax cells. A colony is perennial, i.e. it can survive for many years. Colonies may have up to 30,000 to 50,000 workers. Queens are ¾ inch long. It is black and reddish brown. Honey bees are active spring through summer.

Common Eastern Bumble Bee *Bombus impatiens*

Bumble bees typically nest in the ground in old rodent burrows but can also be found in old birds nests or other cavities. Bumble bees store small amounts of regurgitated nectar in small wax "honey" pots for days they cannot forage. A colony is annual, with only newly fertilized queens surviving until the following spring. Colonies may have up to 500 workers. The Common Eastern Bumble Bee has a yellow thorax with a black spot in the center and a mostly black abdomen except for the yellow first abdominal segment. Note the pollen basket on the hind leg. Bumble bees are commonly seen spring into fall.

Orange-belted Bumble Bee *Bombus ternarius*

Bumble bees are often difficult to identify to species in the field, but the Orange-tailed Bumble bee is the exception to that rule; The two orange abdominal segments really stand out. Sometimes also called the Tricolored Bumble Bee.

Golden Northern Bumble Bee *Bombus fervidus*

Very large and mostly yellow, but with a black band on thorax and black tip on all yellow abdomen. *Bombus borealis* is very similar. Northern U.S. south to Arkansas, North Carolina.

Queen
Male

Small Carpenter Bee *Ceratina species*

Ceratina carpenter bees are metallic dark bluish green, resembling certain halictid bees. Note the pollen on the hind legs. They construct nests by excavating tunnels in pithy stems of shrubs, including sumac and elder. A small carpenter bee is active from May to July.

Digger Bee *Melissodes species*

Pictured is the typical sleeping posture of *Melissodes* long-horned bee species. Males have proportionately very long antennae. These digger bees make underground nests. At the end of long tunnels are "store rooms" loaded with pollen.

♂

Digger Wasps
Family Crabronidae

Members of the Crabronidae were formerly treated as several subfamilies of the Sphecidae (thread-waisted wasps) but were recently raised to family status.

Appearance
More compact and robust than their thread-waisted wasp cousins.

Biology
Most digger wasps dig their own nests in the ground and stock them with insect or spiders. Typically, each species specializes on a specific type of prey including aphids, beetles, bees, true bugs, butterflies, moths, cicadas, cockroaches, flies, grasshoppers, crickets, mantids or spiders. The larvae feed on the cached prey. A few species are kleptoparasitic, feeding their larvae prey that was caught by other wasp species.

American Sand Wasp *Bembix americana spinole*

Keep an eye out for *Bembix americana* in sandy areas such as beaches and sand boxes where they are very gregarious. It is fascinating to watch them digging burrows in sandy slopes (photo series below) where they provision their burrows with captured flies (including large horse flies). Larvae live on the prey. The sand wasps hide the burrow with sand after every visit. They are black with pale yellow bands on the abdomen, resembling yellowjackets. It also has yellow markings on its head and thorax and mostly yellow legs. They are common from June to August.

Bee Wolf *Philanthus ventilabris*

Appropriately, this digger wasp attacks adult bees and provisions its nest with them. Black with yellowish bands on its abdomen, and patches on the head and thorax. It nests in the ground and is common from June to September.

Digger Wasp *Ectemnius species*

Ectemnius wasps are smaller wasps that paralyze flies to cache for their growing larvae. Their nests are usually in twigs in wooded areas, though a few species dig burrows in the soil.

Eastern Cicada Killer *Sphecius speciosus*

It takes a large, robust insect to kill a cicada, and the Cicada Killer is just that. At up to an inch and a half long, it can prey on the large cicadas. Cicada Killers nest in the soil and are quite gregarious, sometimes establishing large aggregations of nests. Look for Cicada Killers during July and August.

Thread-waisted Wasps
Family Sphecidae

Appearance

Most have a smooth body with few hairs and possess short to moderate length antennae. Common colors are black or metallic blue and black with orange or yellow on the legs and abdomen.

Biology

Sphecid wasps are solitary, living in individual nests, although in some species many individuals can live in a small area. Most sphecid wasps nest in the ground, while some nest in cavities, such as in hollow plant stems or cavities in wood, while a few construct nests made of mud. They prey on insects or spiders which they paralyze and feed to their young. They either drag immobilized prey to their nest or they carry them back while they fly. A particular sphecid wasp usually attacks a specific type of insect.

Thread-waisted Wasp   *Isodontia mexicana*

Don't be fooled by its Latin name; this wasp is widespread north of the border...over much of eastern North America! It has even been introduced into Europe. This sphecid wasp provisions its nests in hollow stems with tree crickets and meadow katydids.

Blue Mud Dauber   *Chalybion californicum*

The Blue Mud Dauber is blue (well, actually blue-black with a little iridescence) and it does daub mud (it doesn't gather mud but instead carries water to the abandoned nests of the Black and Yellow Mud Dauber (*Sceliphron caementarium*) and renovates it. A Blue Mud Dauber feeds spiders to its young. It is common from May to August.

Black & Yellow Mud Dauber *Sceliphron caementarium*

Mud balls are formed at moist soil (see photo) and are used to construct the nests of Black and Yellow Mud Daubers. Once the nest is built (often on the sides of homes), it provisions it with spiders to nourish their growing larvae. The Black and Yellow Mud Dauber is black with mostly yellow legs and yellow markings on its thorax. It also has a thin, conspicuous pedicel (actually part of the thorax) connecting the thorax and the abdomen. Their yellow legs dangle in their slow hovering flight. They can be quite common at times. Active from June to August.

Thread-waisted Wasp *Ammophila species*

Warm, sunny, summer days are preferred hunting times for *Ammophila* thread-waisted wasps. They prey on caterpillars (see photos below) and sawfly larvae (which resemble caterpillars) and provision their nests with them. They dig nest burrows in the ground and then temporarily seal them with sand or a pebble just before searching for food. Typically not gregarious, choosing to nest by themselves. They are particularly slender with a long, thin petiole and a black and orange abdomen.

The wasp first drags the captured and immobilized caterpillar back to the underground nest. It then drops the caterpillar so it can remove the pebble from the entrance. (The pebble camouflages the entrance so kleptoparasitic flies can't find it.) The caterpillar is then pulled down into the nest where its young will feed on it.

Golden Digger Wasp *Sphex ichneumoneus*

The Golden Digger Wasp is impressively large and colorful. It has a reddish orange and black abdomen, reddish orange legs and dark wings. It digs a nest in the ground and is usually gregarious, establishing moderate sized congregations. They capture katydids to feed to their young. Look for them from July to September.

Great Black Wasp *Sphex pensylvanicus*

These impressive creatures hunt large long-horned grasshoppers (katydids)—insects much larger than themselves (see photos). Their nest is provisioned with the katydids, providing food for the developing young.

In these two photographs we can see how the Great Black Wasp is able to capture, grasp and fly off with prey much larger than itself. In this case it is a *Neoconcephalus* species of katydid.

Cuckoo Wasps
Family Chrysididae

Appearance
Bright metallic green or blue with sculptured bodies. Underside of abdomens concave which allows them to curls their bodies into balls.

Biology
Common around flowers. They parasitize various bee and wasp larvae, especially solitary species. June to August.

Cuckoo Wasp *Family Chrysididae*

Cuckoo wasps are often iridescent green with thousands of tiny "punctures" all over their head, abdomen and thorax. Females search out solitary bees or wasps in order to deposit eggs, one at a time, into their brood cells. The larvae feed on the host bee or its cached food.

Velvet Ants
Family Mutillidae

Appearance
Females resemble stout ants. Males possess wings and are sometimes larger than females. Often red or orange.

Biology
Found in dry, sandy areas where vegetation is sparse. Parasitize various ground nesting wasps or bees. Females search the ground; males visit flowers. The females can administer a painful sting.

Velvet Ant *Dasymutilla species*

Though not common in the North Woods, velvet ants are too unique to ignore. This species frenetically searches sandy areas for the nests of sand wasps. Females are wingless and resemble ants (see photo) while males have wings and look more like the wasps they are.

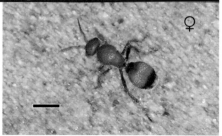

Ants
Family Formicidae

Appearance

Very small to moderate in size, measuring about ¹/₂₀ to ¹/₂ inch long. The anterior part of the abdomen is narrowed to form one or two nodes or bumps. Many ants are brown or black while some are yellow and some species are black and red. Workers are wingless while reproductive females and males are winged when they emerge from pupae.

Biology

Ants are social insects forming colonies that are typically found in the ground either exposed or under objects, like stones or logs while others can be found in rotted wood. Colonies can number from dozens to thousands. Ants feed on a variety of foods including insects, nectar, honeydew, and human food. Newly mated females found new nests after mating swarms of flying males and females leave their nests. The males die shortly afterwards. Females remove their wings after mating and landing. Ants are common from spring into fall. Some species can even be found during the winter when they nest inside buildings.

New York Carpenter Ant *Camponotus noveboracensis*

Contrary to popular belief, carpenter ants do not eat wood—yes, they do chew wood to make nesting cavities (see photo below), but they eat living and dead insects, honeydew and many human foods. This carpenter ant nests in standing dead trees or in logs. It has a black head and shiny abdomen and a reddish thorax (many carpenters ants are just dull black) and petiole with a single node. The evenly rounded thorax has a single node. Mating swarms occur from April through June.

This cross-section of a tree trunk show the vertical burrows of the carpenter ants. It also shows the chiseled cavity of a Pileated Woodpecker trying to get at the ants.

Mound-building Ant *Formica species*

A worker can be black, brown, red or combination. They prefer honeydew but will also eat live and dead insects. They build nests in exposed sites with some species constructing large mounds (below). Mating swarms occur July through September.

False Honey Ant *Prenolepis imparis*

A False Honey Ant is brown, with a one-segmented node and particularly long antennae. They feed on honeydew and flower nectar and nests in the soil, especially in open, well shaded sites. They are also occasionally nest under concealed objects, such as stones, logs, or concrete. They swarm in April and May.

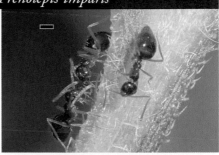

Pavement Ant *Tetramorium caespitum*

A pavement ant worker is about 1/8 inch long, is reddish brown to black, and has a petiole with two nodes. It prefers a variety of foods including insects as well as human food such as meats, pet food, sweets, bread, and nuts. Pavement ants nest in the soil under objects including stones and logs as well as under sidewalks and driveways. Mating swarms occur from May through July.

Spider Wasps
Family Pompilidae

Appearance

Medium to large slender wasps, most ranging in size from 1/2 to one inch long. Spider wasps have long spiny legs and medium length antennae that is held curled by the females. They are typically black or dark blue often with dark-colored wings, which are sometimes spotted. As they move about on flowers or on the ground they constantly flick their wings in a seemingly nervous fashion.

A spider wasp frenetically searches for spiders on a sandy patch.

This captured and paralyzed orbweaver spider will become a meal for the developing spider wasp larva.

Biology

Spider wasps are solitary wasps that typically live in nests in the ground while others make nests in cells of mud or rotted wood. Spider wasps feed their young spiders they capture, paralyze, and bring to their nests. There is one egg per spider. Spider wasps are common throughout the summer. Spider wasps can inflict a painful sting to people.

Spider Wasp *Episyron biguttatus*

Look out orbweaver spiders! *Episyron biguttatus* frenetically searches for, and captures, orbweaver spiders (family Araneidae) to provision its nest, which is typically in sandy areas or in gravel banks. This spider wasp is black with a pair of small white spots on its abdomen. It is common from July into August.

Gasteruptiid Wasps
Family Gasteruptiidae

Appearance

Slender, medium sized insects with moderate length antennae and the head attached to a distinctive, slender neck. The abdomen is attached to the top of the thorax. Gasteruptiid wasps have gray or black bodies marked with orange or brown.

Biology

Gasteruptiid wasps are common around flowers, such as wild parsnip, wild carrots, and related plants. They are also found around logs, stumps, and twigs where certain solitary wasps and bees nest. Gasteruptiid wasp larvae either parasitize the larvae of these solitary wasps or bees or feed on food that has been provisioned for their hosts' larvae. Gasteruptiid wasps are common from June to August.

Gasteruptiid Wasp *Gasteruption species*

The abdomen of Gasteruptiid wasps is held so high, and at such an angle, as to appear to spring from the top of the thorax! Also note the "neck" connecting the head to the thorax. Females have an ovipositor to lay eggs in the larvae of solitary bees or wasps.

Yellowjackets, Hornets, Paper Wasps, Mason Wasps & Potter Wasps Family Vespidae

Appearance

Relatively smooth insects with few hairs and narrow wings folded over their back when at rest. Vespid wasps have elbowed antennae.

Biology

Many vespid wasps are social, insects constructing nests that survive one season. Only newly mated queens survive the winter and start new nests in the spring. Other species are solitary. Typically vespids make their nests from chewed wood fibers, while others construct their nests from mud or clay. Vespid wasps prey on a variety of insects (sometimes spiders) to feed their young. They often possess a stinger which can be used repeatedly. Vespid wasps are commonly seen from spring into the fall.

Aerial Yellowjacket   *Dolichovespula arenia*

An Aerial Yellowjacket worker has a black thorax with yellow markings and a black and yellow striped abdomen. It is a social wasp, nesting out in the open anywhere from near the ground to tall trees as well as on buildings (nest detail: right photo). An aerial yellowjacket is active from spring into the fall.

Bald-faced Hornet   *Dolichovespula maculata*

A Bald-faced Hornet (actually a type of yellowjacket) is mostly black with whitish markings. It is a social wasp usually constructing its paper nest high off the ground, often from the branches of trees (right). Bald-faced Hornets are active from spring until fall. Colonies can number several thousand workers.

Potter Wasp *Eumenes fraternus*

This solitary wasp has a black body with whitish markings on its head, thorax and abdomen and violet colored wings. The abdomen has a constriction between the long, narrow first second and the second. A potter wasp is well named, as they construct pot-shaped nests made of clay. It provisions its nest with moth and leaf beetle larvae. Common from June into September.

Northern Paper Wasp *Polistes fuscatus*

A paper wasp is slender-bodied with relatively long legs. It is dark brown with yellow stripes and two orange spots on its abdomen, but color pattern can vary greatly. It constructs in nest on horizontal surfaces, like branches on human structures, like the eaves of a home. Paper wasps prey on moth and butterfly caterpillars and are common from spring into fall. Colonies number up to a couple dozen workers or more.

Eastern Yellowjacket *Vespula maculifrons*

An Eastern Yellowjacket worker has a black body and yellowish markings and a black and yellow striped abdomen. Very similar to *Dolichovespula arenia* but note the dark umbrella-shaped mark on the front of the abdomen. It is a social wasp nesting in the ground in the ground in types of sites, including hardwood forests, ditches, and yards. You do not actually see the nest, just an entrance where the workers fly back and forth. An eastern yellowjacket is common from spring into fall.

Caddisflies
Order Trichoptera

Diversity
There are 26 families and 1556 species in North America. Caddisflies are very common in the North Woods.

Appearance
Adults: Small to medium-sized moth-like insects with very long antennae, commonly as long or longer than their bodies. Their four wings, covered with short, fine hairs, are held tent-like over their abdomens. These wings are similarly-sized and shaped to each other. Caddisflies possess mouthparts with conspicuous palps; the mandibles are absent or highly reduced. Most have a short, stubby proboscis. Many caddisflies are brownish or otherwise dull-colored.

Larvae: Small to medium-sized caterpillar-like insects with cylindrical-shaped bodies. Caddisfly larvae have conspicuous heads with chewing mouthparts and possess short peg-like antennae. They possess conspicuous legs behind their heads on their thoraxes but lack prolegs, i.e. false legs, on their abdomens, except for the pair at the very end. The abdomen often bears filament-like gills.

Habitats
Immature caddisflies are found in essentially all fresh water environments, including streams, ponds, lakes and even temporary pools of water. They prefer cool, running water, although some species take advantage of warm, still aquatic environments. Adults are weak flyers and are generally found near water. Adults are active at night and can be commonly found around lights.

Life Cycle
Caddisfly larvae are holometabolous insects, using complete metamorphosis to develop. Adults lay eggs in the water often on objects, like stones, or on nearby sites, such as overhanging branches. Caddisfly larvae can generally be divided into one of three groups: case-makers, net-makers and free living. All caddisfly larvae have the ability to make silk using modified glands on their heads which they use for building cases, nets, retreats and cocoons.

Case-makers make little shelters our of objects on hand (see following pages). Net-making caddisflies employ a different strategy. Found in swift moving water, they construct silken nets which collects food the currents bring to them. The larvae stay nearby in retreats while waiting for food. Free-living caddisfly larvae do not make cases, nets, or retreats. Instead they actively search for food among rocks or other objects in moving water. They make a dome-like silken case only when they pupate.

Larvae pupate in the water, often under stones or logs. As they complete metamorphosis, the pupae swim to the surface and crawl to shore where the adults emerge. Caddisflies in the North Woods typically take one year to develop.

Food

Many larval caddisflies are scavengers, feeding on decaying organic debris that they encounter in the water. Others are plant feeders, consuming algae and diatoms while some caddisfly larvae are predacious, eating small aquatic invertebrate animals, like black fly larvae. Some adult caddisflies may feed on liquids but most probably do not feed.

Water Quality

Although some caddisfly species are tolerant of polluted water, most require clean water, making this insect group important when determining water quality.

Don't confuse them with...

...moths and butterflies. Moths and butterflies possess scales on their wings which they hold flat or straight up and down when at rest. They possess coiled, tube-like mouthparts and their antennae are much shorter than their bodies. Moth and butterfly larvae possess prolegs, i.e. fleshy false legs on their abdomens. Moth and butterfly larvae are rarely aquatic.

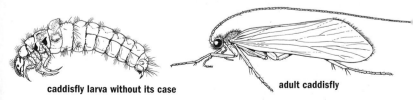

caddisfly larva without its case   adult caddisfly

Caddisfly Larval Cases

The case-making caddisflies are renown as architects for the distinctive and unique cases they construct. Caddisflies use an array of different types of materials to construct these shelters, especially sand, leaves and small pieces of wood. These cases take on a wide array of shapes, such as tube-like, saddle-like, snail shell-like and turtle shell-like. These cases are portable, allowing the larvae to move about as they look for food.

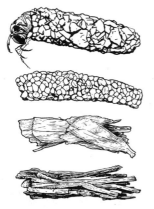

examples of larval cases

Top: *Platycentropus radiatus*; middle two: *Phryganea* species; bottom: possibly *Limnephilus* species.

Long-horned Caddisfly *Family Leptoceridae*

Extremely long antennae may be the first clue that this is not a moth nor a lacewing. Adults usually seen after sundown; sometimes at lights. Larvae make "log cabin" cases out of tiny twigs or make a case of leaf and stem parts.

Black Dancer   *Mystacides sepulchralis*

The Black Dancer is a tiny long-horned caddisfly. They are recognized by their very long, slender antennae which are about twice the length of their bodies. Metallic blue-black with red eyes. The larva is associated with shallow areas of lakes and ponds as well as slow currents of rivers. It constructs a slender case made from sand and plant material with evergreen needles or twigs commonly extending beyond the front end of the case. Adults are seen from June through August. Unlike most caddisflies, the Black Dancer is active during early morning and evening.

Zebra Caddisfly   *Macrostemum zebratum*

Large fast rivers with lots of silt and organic material is where you are most likely to find the Zebra Caddisfly (although small, fast, clean streams are also utilized). It is a type of net-spinning caddisfly which is a large, common group of insects. The "Zebra" in its common name refers to the black stripes on its brown wings. The larva which grows as large as 2/3 inch does not construct a case but builds a net amongst rocks which catches tiny bits of organic material, phytoplankton and bacteria for it to eat. The larva rests nearby in a tube-like silken retreat. Watch for Zebra Caddisfly adults in June and July.

Northern Casemaker Caddisfly   *Nemotaulius hostilis*

This species is one of the larger caddisflies in the North Woods, measuring up to an inch in length from its head to the end of its wings. The northern casemaker caddisfly belongs to a large group of caddisflies that are primarily found in the northern U.S. The northern casemaker caddisfly larva can grow to over an inch in size. It constructs a flat log cabin type case made from pieces of leaves and twigs. The larva feeds primarily on decaying bits of plant material and occasionally live plant matter and diatoms. This species commonly develops in lakes, ponds, marshes, as well as slow moving streams. Adults are found from late May to late June.

Butterflies & Moths
Order Lepidoptera

Diversity

There are 80 families and over 11,000 species in North America, making this group one of the largest insect orders. Butterflies and moths are very common in the North Woods.

Appearance

Adults: Lepidoptera have four wings, often large, nearly always completely covered with scales, although there are a few cases where scales are lacking. Butterflies and moths have slender, sucking mouthparts that are coiled underneath their head when not in use.

Larvae: Typically, cylindrical-shaped with a conspicuous head, chewing mouthparts, six true legs, and two to five pairs of prolegs on the abdomen. Leaf miners and aquatic larvae are modified for their unusual lifestyles. Their bodies may appear smooth or covered with many hairs or spines.

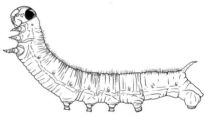

caterpillar

Habitats

Adult butterflies and moths are found in all terrestrial habitats in the North Woods. Butterflies are typically daytime flyers and are commonly found on flowers and foliage. Most moths are nocturnal and are attracted to lights. However, clearwing moths, hawkmoths and others are both nocturnal and daytime flyers. The Virginia Ctenucha is often found nectaring alongside monarchs at milkweeds in mid-late summer.

Larvae (caterpillars) can be found in many different terrestrial microhabitats. Some species hide in leaf litter or under bark during the day. Others create temporary feeding and hiding shelters by gluing leaf parts together with silk.

Life Cycle

Butterflies and moths are holometabolous insects, using complete metamorphosis to develop. Butterflies and moths typically have one or two generations in a year. Butterflies form a chrysalis, a pupa without an outside covering; whereas moths form a cocoon, a pupa surrounded by an outside silken covering.

Food

Butterflies and moths typically feed on nectar, although they are also known to feed on sap and other liquids. Puddling is a behavior where butterflies (and some moths) congregate and appear to feed on damp soil at the edges of a shallow water body to obtain salts concentrated through evaporation. Coprophagy (feeding at feces) can also be observed. Butterflies are obtaining protein and salts by regurgitating saliva onto the feces and then reimbibing. The larvae of many species typically feed on living plants, primarily leaves,. Some are borers in twigs, stems or wood or leaf miners. Others (lichen moths, ermines and some noctuids) specialize on fungus or lichens as larvae.

Don't confuse them with...

...adult wasps. You can distinguish between clearwing moths (Sesiidae) and stinging wasps as the wasps have a clearly constricted "wasp waist." Sessiids have thicker bodies and different coloration than yellow jackets or paper wasps.

...larval sawflies. You can distinguish between them as sawflies have pro-legs on nearly all abdominal segments.

...hummingbirds. Hawkmoths feeding at hummingbird feeders or large hibiscus flowers confuse some bird watchers. Hawkmoths have antennae whereas hummingbirds do not.

Further your knowledge

In a book of this scope we can only cover so many species. If you want to look further into the world of the "leps," pick up copies of Kollath-Stensaas's field guides to the butterflies and moths of the North Woods. The comprehensive butterfly guide has range maps and phenograms for all species.

A guide to all 125 North Woods butterflies by Minnesota naturalist Larry Weber.
Butterflies of the North Woods: 2nd Edition
ISBN: 978-0-9673793-5-7

A guide to over 300 North Woods moths by Minnesota biologist Jim Sogaard.
Moths & Caterpillars of the North Woods
ISBN: 978-0-9792006-6-3

Swallowtails
Family Papilionidae

Appearance

Medium to large sized butterflies with wingspan varying from 2 5/8 to five inches. Typically have dark-colored wings with yellow markings or yellow wings with black markings with a long conspicuous tail on each hind wing.

Puddling Canadian Tiger Swallowtails are taking up moisture and minerals from wet soil. Often witnessed in June.

Biology

Swallowtails lay their eggs on a variety of herbaceous and hardwood trees and shrubs. They overwinter as a chrysalis. Look for swallowtails adults and from May to August.

Canadian Tiger Swallowtail *Papilio canadensis*

This is the common yellow swallowtail in the North Woods. To differentiate from the Eastern Tiger Swallowtail note the solid yellow band on the trailing edge of the forewing's undersides. Wingspan to 3 1/2 inches. Often seen puddling in groups of a dozen or more in June. Adults fly May to mid July.

Black Swallowtail *Papilio polyxene*

Not nearly as common as the Canadian Tiger Swallowtail, but just as spectacular. Wingspan 2 5/8 to 3 1/2 inches. Mostly black with a series of yellow spots on all wings and blue spots on the hind wings as well as a small red eyespot. Found in open fields, meadows and gardens where it lays eggs on plants in the carrot family including dill, parsley, carrots, celery and Queen's Anne lace. Adults are common May and June and again from July into September.

Whites & Sulphurs
Family Pieridae

Appearance

Small to moderate sized butterflies with a body length typically between $5/16$ to $3/4$ inch long and a wingspan of $1^{1}/8$ to two inches. They usually have white, yellow, or orange wings, often with black markings.

Large groups of sulphurs congregate at wet soil to drink and take in minerals.

Biology

Whites and sulphurs lay their eggs on a variety of herbaceous plants, especially in the mustard and legume families. Whites and sulphurs overwinter as a chrysalis and are seen May into October.

Clouded Sulphur *Colias philodice*

The males' wings are yellow while the females' are greenish white. Found in meadows and fields where it lays its eggs on alfalfa, clover, vetch and other legumes. Can be common at mud puddles taking in moisture and minerals with its proboscis (photo above). May into October.

Cabbage White *Pieris rapae*

The Cabbage White has white wings; the forewings each have a black tip and one (male) or two (female) black dots. Common in fields and gardens where it lays its eggs on cabbage, nasturtiums, broccoli and other plants in the mustard family. It is common at mud puddles drinking moisture. May into September.

Coppers, Hairstreaks & Blues Family Lycaenidae

Appearance

Small, fragile butterflies with a slender body ¼ to ½ inch long and a wingspan of ⅝ to 1 ⅜ inches wide. Their wings are typically orange and black, brown, or blue, sometimes with small tails on their hind wings. Their antennae often have small white rings on them and their eyes are usually encircled by white scales.

Biology

Gossamer-winged butterflies are associated with a wide variety of herbaceous and deciduous trees and shrubs. Some species have a wide host range while are others are much narrower in their preferences. The larvae of many these butterflies are attractive to ants as they secrete a sugary substance the ants feed on. Gossamer-winged butterflies are common spring and summer.

Spring Azure *Celastrina argiolus*

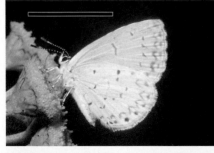

It has pale blue wings without tails with small black markings on the forward edge of the forewings. It is found in moist wooded sites where it lays eggs on dogwoods, viburnums, and other plants and is found. A spring azure is found May and June (a closely related species, the summer azure occurs July into September).

Harvester *Feniseca tarquinius*

This tiny sprite sticks close to alder thickets and other damp areas. Its caterpillar is carnivorous on woolly aphids (which are also found on alder). Does not visit flowers but takes up salts and other minerals from dung, carrion, damp soil or even your salty skin! Also takes honeydew from aphids. May to August.

American Copper *Lycaena phlaenas americana*

The forewings are orange with black spots and a border along the forward edge. The hind wings are gray brown with a narrow orange band. They are found in fields and other open areas and lay their eggs on sheep sorrel and curly dock. They have two generations and are seen spring and summer.

Bog Copper *Lycaena epixanthe*

A very northern butterfly whose range is limited to that of its host plant, cranberry. Male has purple sheen to upper forewings with few black spots (Dorcas Copper and Purplish Copper have more). Undersides whitish in North Woods (inset photo). Slow and low flight. Flies mainly in July; in Black Spruce bogs with cranberry.

Coral Hairstreak *Satyrum titus*

Brushy fields, forest edges, meadows and roadsides are where you can find this delightful hairstreak. The striking row of coral spots on the hindwing below is distinctive. Caterpillars feed on the leaves of chokecherries, juneberries and wild plum.

Banded Hairstreak *Satyrum calanus*

The Banded Hairstreak shows an intricate pattern of small white and black dashes on the underside of the wings as well as a small blue and orange spots. A small tail on each hind wing. Never perches with open wings. Found in wooded areas and adjacent open sites where it lays eggs on oak, walnut and hickory. June into August.

Brush-footed Butterflies Family Nymphalidae

Appearance

Moderate to large butterflies with a body length of 3/8 to 1 1/4 inch long and a wingspan ranging from 1 to 4 inches. Many have orange and black wings, although it varies as others are brown or brown and yellow. The front legs of brush-footed butterflies are reduced; these butterflies use just their second and third pair of legs to walk.

Biology

Brush-footed butterflies lay their eggs on a wide variety of woody tree and shrubs and herbaceous plants. They overwinter either as larvae or adults. You can see brush-footed butterflies from early spring into the fall.

Great Spangled Fritillary *Speyeria cybele*

The largest North Woods fritillary with a wingspan up to 3 1/4 inches. It has orange wings with brown near the body and a series of black markings. This butterfly is common in fields and open woodlands. It lays eggs on or near violet leaves in the summer which hatch in the fall. It spends the winter as a young larva. Found late June into September.

Atlantis Fritillary *Speyeria atlantis*

A larger northern fritillary with a distinctive under wing pattern. Usually seen nectaring along dirt roads, woodland openings, forest edges and moist meadows; often in small groups. Wingspan ranges from 2 to 2 3/4 inches.

Silvery Checkerspot *Chlosyne nycteis*

It is orange with a black border and black markings including a row of small black spots on the hind wings. It is typically found in damp woodlands and meadows where it lays eggs on sunflowers, asters, Black-eyed Susans and other plants. The Silvery Checkerspot overwinters as a larva. Look for it June and July.

Northern Crescent *Phyciodes selenis*

Very common butterfly that is often seen perched on the ground with wings spread open. Places to look for this species would include dirt roads, boat launches, meadows and streamsides. Open orange area on hindwings above. Orange-tipped antennae.

Eastern Comma *Polygonia comma*

One of our hibernating butterflies. In fall, it finds a sheltered spot to spend the winter. Glycerol, a natural antifreeze floods the body, allowing them to freeze solid and live again in spring. They feed on sap. The summer form has a darker border than the winter form. Lays eggs on nettles, false nettles, hops and elm. Flies April and May and again from late June into the fall.

Milbert's Tortoiseshell *Nymphalis milberti*

Another of our butterflies that hibernates as an adult. Eggs laid in large clusters on Stinging Nettle. May emerge from hibernation as early as late March. In early spring, Milbert's must feed on oozing maple and birch sap and dung to get required nutrients. Wingspan to 2 1/4 inches. Flies March to October (two broods).

Mourning Cloak *Nymphalis antiopa*

A real harbinger of spring. Adults hibernate but awaken in April and can be seen on nice warm, sunny days. Wingspan of 3 to 4 inches. Lays eggs on willow and poplar as well as elm, birch and hackberry. It overwinters as an adult and Watch for mourning cloaks from April into October.

Painted Lady *Vanessa cardui*

Because they can't survive northern winters, the Painted Lady migrates north from Mexico and California each spring and lays eggs on thistle, sunflower, burdock, Pearly Everlasting and other herbaceous plants. Wingspan to 2 $1/4$ inches. Look for the Painted Lady from May through September.

Red Admiral *Vanessa atalanta*

Adults may hibernate but also migrate. The under wings are equally colorful but with blues and pinks. It lays eggs on nettles, false nettles and wood nettles. Wingspan of 1 $3/8$ to 2 $1/4$ inches. Adult flies mid April to mid October in the North Woods.

White Admiral *Limenitis arthemis arthemis*

It is found in open hardwood forests and forest edges where it lays eggs on hardwood trees and shrubs including aspen, birch and basswood. It overwinters as a larva on its host food. Wingspan 2 to 3 inches. Looks for the White Admiral from May into September.

Common Wood-Nymph *Cercyonis pegala*

Contrary to its name, the Common Wood-Nymph is rarely found in shaded woods. It is more common in sunny places such as brushy fields, marshes, roadsides and the edges of woods. Unlike other satyrs, it can often be found nectaring on flowers. Wingspan 2 to 3 inches. Late June to late August in the North Woods.

Northern Pearly-eye *Enodia anthedon*

Shaded deciduous woods is where you'll find the Pearly-eye; often near swamps and streams. Adults forego nectar and instead feed on sap from willows, birches and aspens. Aggressively territorial; dart after intruders, returning to their tree-trunk perch. Wingspan to 2 1/2 inches. Mid June to mid August.

Jutta Arctic *Oenis jutta*

While not a common butterfly, it certainly is a species indicative of the boreal forest. Look for them fluttering through open Black Spruce bogs with mature trees. They nearly disappear as they land on the rough spruce trunks, wings folded and head down. Mainly fly in June, but many populations only fly every other year.

Monarch *Danaus plexipus*

Monarch are one of the few butterflies that migrate during fall, traveling to the mountains of Mexico. The first migrants return in June; fly south in September. Lays its eggs on milkweed. Two broods occur with June caterpillars emerging as adults by mid-July and the second brood in August or early September. Wingspan up to 4 inches.

Skippers
Family Hesperidae

Appearance

Small to medium size stout-bodied insects with a wingspan of 7/8 to 1 2/3 inches wide. Often brown with whitish or orange markings, which are held at different angles when at rest. The antennae have hooked tips.

Biology

Larvae often inconspicuously feed inside rolled leaves. Skippers are often found on flowers or perched on foliage and are common June and July.

Dun Skipper *Euphyes vestris*

Uniformly dark brown wings above with two pale spots below forewings. It is found in moist areas and open woodlands where it lays its eggs on sedges. Look for this skipper from late June to late August.

Hobomok Skipper *Poanes hobomok*

Look for the large pale yellowish orange patch on the undersides of the hindwings. Found along roadsides, in meadows, along woodland paths and many other places. It lays its eggs on grasses. Flies as early as mid May and as late as mid July.

Arctic Skipper *Carterocephalus palaemon*

Not strictly Arctic, nonetheless this boldly marked skipper's range is very northern. The large silvery white spots on the UNDERSIDES of its wings are its most conspicuous feature. Found in moist areas and open woodlands where it lays its eggs on sedges. Mid May to mid July.

Sphinx Moths
Family Sphingidae

Appearance

Moderate to large sized heavy bodied moths with long narrow forewings and wingspans between one and 4 ¾ inches. Hind wings may be brightly colored. A few lack scales over part of the wings.

Biology

While most sphinx moths fly at night, a few are active during the day, especially at dusk. Because of their size and the ability to hover, these species are sometimes confused as hummingbirds.

White-lined Sphinx *Hyles lineata*

Any "hummingbird" seen at dusk hovering at your garden flowers may be this moth. They are large (wingspan to 3 inches) and the wings make a loud humming sound in flight. Occasionally fly during midday. Mid May to early October.

Big Poplar Sphinx *Pachysphinx modesta*

Well named—it's big and the caterpillar feeds on poplar. Wingspan of 3 ½ to 4 ¾ inches. The hind wings are mostly reddish with a small, bluish triangular-shaped spot. Lays its eggs on poplar and willow. Adults fly late May through July.

One-eyed Sphinx *Smerinthus cerisyi*

A One-eyed Sphinx of course has two eyes; the name refers to the single eyespot (complete with pupil) on each hind wing. Wingspan of 2 ⅜ to 3 inches. Unique perching posture (inset). Found in forests and woodlands where it lays it eggs on poplar, willow, and plum. Adults fly May into July.

Giant Silk Moths
Family Saturniidae

Appearance

Medium to large stout-bodied moths with a body length of $3/4$ to $1\ 7/8$ inch long and a wingspan of one to six inches. They are often colorful and strikingly marked. Giant silk moths have feather-like antennae; in the males they are broadly so while in females they are more narrow.

Biology

Giant silkworm moths lay their eggs on a variety of hardwood trees and shrubs. Different species may have a narrow or broad host range. Giant silkworm moths typically pass the winter as pupae. Watch for these moths from May to August.

Rosy Maple Moth *Dryocampa rubicunda*

This moth gets noticed by home-owners when attracted to their outdoor lights at night. Wingspan up to 2 inches. The forewings are pale to bright yellow, with pinkish to lavender. The hind wings are a pale yellow. Found in forests where it lays it eggs on maple, box elder and occasionally oak. Overwinters as a pupa. June to August.

Io Moth *Automeris io*

Sexually dimorphic; the male (pictured here) has bright yellow forewings while the female's are reddish brown. Hindwings are yellow with a large blue eyespot on each. Wingspan is $1\ 7/8$ to $2\ 7/8$ inches. Found in wooded areas as well as fields. Lays eggs on aspen, birch, blackberry, clover, oak, poplar and grass. Common June and July.

Polyphemus Moth *Antheraea polyphemus*

Nearly as large as the Cecropia below, with a wingspan of 3 3/4 to 5 1/4 inches. It has brown wings with a large blue and yellow eyespot on each hind wing. Typically found around wooded areas, laying eggs on a variety of trees and shrubs, such as ash, birch, maple, oak and willow. Polyphemus moths are active May into July.

Cecropia Moth *Hyalophora cecropia*

Huge, with wingspan from 4 to 5 3/4 inches. White and reddish brown lines running through both wings and a white comma-shaped outlined in reddish brown on the hind wings. Lives in woodlands where it lays it eggs on a variety of hardwood trees including, linden, maple, box elder, elm, oak, birch, and poplar. Can be very common in suburbia too. Overwinters as a cocoon. May into July.

Luna Moth *Actias luna*

Always a treat to see, the Luna is stunning in its size (wingspan of 4 inches) and color (minty green with purple accents). Also shows an eyespot on each hind wing. Most people first see them at their porch lights in the morning (if they've been left on all night). Caterpillar feeds on birch (*Betula* spp.). May and June.

Promethea Moth *Callosamia promethea*

Dimorphic, with males mostly brown and females reddish brown. Caterpillars feed on many types of trees and shrubs. Adults do not feed. Usually it is just the females that are attracted to lights. Adults on the wing in June and July.

Inchworms & Geometers Family Geometridae

Appearance

Small to medium sized moths with a wingspan of about ³/₈ to 2 ³/₄ inches. The wings are broad, often with wavy lines on them. Males and females of the same species can vary in color. Some females are even wingless.

Biology

Eggs laid on a wide variety of trees and shrubs where the caterpillars feed on leaves or needles. Overwinter either as eggs or larvae. Active spring and summer and sometimes into fall.

White-striped Black *Trichodosia albovittata*

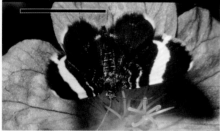

Boldly marked black wings with a white band running across the forewings. Flies during the day in woodlands where it lays its eggs on impatiens. A White-striped Black flies is active June to August.

Pale Beauty *Campaea perlata*

Truly a pale beauty; pale grayish white to pale green. It is found in woodlands and forests where it lays eggs on trees and shrubs including aspen, birch, oak, rose, cherry, willow as well as fir. Overwinters as a caterpillar. Watch for adults in late July and August.

Sharp-lined Yellow *Sicya macularia*

Bright yellow and brown forewings and pale white hind wings with a pale yellow area. It lays its eggs on a variety of hardwood trees and shrubs, such as birch, ash and alder. This moth is present July and August.

Crocus Geometer *Xanthotype species*

Often day-flying but *Xanthotype* moths will also come to light at night. Caterpillar foods include Poison Ivy and many other broadleaved plants. Often seen in Black Spruce bogs.

Large Lace-border Moth *Scopula limboundata*

Whitish to yellowish with three wavy lines running through the wings and often a lace-like pattern along the margin of hind wings. Eggs laid on a variety of plants, including apple, elm, blackberry, cherry, dandelion and clover. Commonly found June and July.

Hooktip Moths Family Drepanidae

Appearance

Moderate sized moths with a wingspan of one to 1 1/2 inches. The forewings are sickle-shaped and generally yellowish to brownish, sometimes with reddish brown.

Biology

Hooktip moths lay their eggs on a variety of trees and shrub where the larvae feed on the leaves from a loosely tied shelter. They overwinter as pupae in leaves on the ground. Watch for them from June to August.

Arched Hooktip Moth *Drepana arcuata*

An Arched Hooktip Moth is yellowish to brownish wings with distinctive wavy black lines on the forewings. The tips of the forewings are particularly hooked looking. It lays it eggs on birch and alder. Look for it June to August.

Tiger Moths
Family Arctiidae

Appearance

Small to medium sized moths with medium to stout bodies $1/4$ to $7/8$ inch long. They have a wingspan ranging from one to $2 3/4$ inches. The forewings often are brightly colored white, red, or white and conspicuously striped or spotted. Tiger moths typically hold their wings tent-like over bodies.

Biology

Tiger moths are associated with a wide variety of herbaceous and hardwood trees and shrubs. In the north woods, our species are typically generalists consuming a wide range of plants. Many tiger moths overwinter as partially developed larvae or as pupae. Adults are commonly found spring and summer.

Virginia Ctenucha *Ctenucha virginica*

Day-flying and striking. It has chocolate brown wings; the forewings are usually slightly darker, an orange head and a blue thorax and abdomen. Found in moist fields and meadows where it lays it eggs on different grasses. Look for adults in June and July nectaring at milkweed flowers.

Black & Yellow Lichen Moth *Lychomorpha pholus*

Who is mimicking who? The Black and Yellow Lichen Moth greatly resembles the End Band Net-winged Beetle (see page 103). More black and orange than black and yellow. Found in wooded areas and adjacent open areas where it flies during the day. It lays eggs on lichen. July to September.

Great Tiger Moth *Arctia caja*

A beautiful moth and a great find if you see one. This is a true boreal moth that ranges around the globe in taiga and boreal forests. The photo doesn't show their stunning orange hindwings that are dotted with blue spots encircled in black. Sometimes comes to lights. Flies late July to early August.

Parthenice Tiger Moth *Grammia parthenice*

Tiger moths are highly sought after by moth enthusiasts; they are boldly marked, colorful and sometimes uncommon. The Parthenice Tiger Moth has wonderful black and tan geometric patterns on its fore wings and orange hindwings with black triangles. It is on the wing from mid July to August.

Leconte's Haploa *Haploa lecontei*

Forewings are cream-colored to white with dark brown margins in varying patterns; the hind wings are typically white. These tiger moths are found in woodlands and adjacent sites where they feed on a wide variety of herbaceous plants, as well as woody plants. Overwinter as caterpillars; look for adults June to August.

Prominents
Family Notodontidae

Appearance

Moderate sized moths with a medium body ranging in length from 3/8 to 1¼ inch. They Their wings are usually brown or yellow with a wingspan of 3/4 to 2 3/8 inch. These moths often have a tuft of hair on their thorax projecting backwards.

Biology

Prominents and oakworms lay their eggs on a variety of hardwood trees and shrub where the larvae feed on the leaves. They generally overwinter as pupae and are seen from June to August.

Sigmoid Prominent *Clostera albosigma*

Note the interesting wing pattern that mimics the dark shadow of a crinkled leaf. Perches with front legs held out in front. Caterpillar feeds mainly on aspens and willows.

Red-washed Prominent *Oligocentria semirufescens*

The Red-washed Prominent's unique perching style is an effective camouflage; essentially mimicking a broken branch. Its wings are rolled and head down. Caterpillar feeds on poplar and willow.

Tent Caterpillars & Lappet Moths Family Lasiocampidae

Appearance

Medium sized moths with stout hairy bodies. When resting, these moths often place their first pair of legs forward and its second pair of legs straight out at a 90 degree angle.

Biology

Associated with a variety of hardwood trees and shrubs where the caterpillars feed on leaves. These moths overwinter as eggs or larvae and are commonly seen spring and summer, and occasionally into fall.

The caterpillar of the tent caterpillar is a common and unwelcome sight to homeowners during outbreaks.

Lappet Moth *Phyllodesma americana*

Wings are reddish brown with a grayish margin. A lappet moth is found in wooded areas; it lays its eggs on a variety of trees and shrubs, such as birch, apple, alder, oak, and poplar. A lappet moth overwinters as a pupa; moths are present May to July.

Eastern Forest Tent Caterpillar *Malacosoma disstria*

Better known (and hated) in its larval stage, the Eastern Forest Tent Caterpillar occasionally erupts in massive outbreaks, often stripping aspen forests bare of leaves and swarming over houses. Fortunately it has a cyclical life cycle, occurring in very low numbers at first, gradually increasing for about 8 to 13 years. Their populations

eventually build to tremendously large numbers for about 3 to 5 years before their numbers crash and the cycle repeats itself. Wings are yellowish to reddish brown with two dark lines running through them. A forest tent caterpillar overwinters in the egg stage; adult moths are active July and August.

Owlet Moths
Family Noctuidae

Appearance

Small to moderate moths, usually medium to stout-bodied between $1/2$ to 1 $1/4$ inches long. They typically have a wingspan ranging from 1 to 3 $3/4$ inches. They have moderately narrowed forewings and broad hind wings.

Biology

The habits of noctuid moths vary considerably. Some are leaf feeders, others are borers, while some chew stems, i.e. cutworms. Noctuid moths generally pupate in the soil or leaf litter. Common spring and summer.

Eight-spotted Forester *Alypia octomaculata*

Eight spots; two pale yellow spots on each forewing and two white spots on each hind wing. Note the orange tufts of hair on the first two pairs of legs that differentiate this noctuid moth from a very similar pyralid moth. Found in woodlands where it lays eggs on grape and Virginia creeper. May into July.

Sweetheart Underwing *Catocala amatrix*

A rather drab moth until it reveals its hind wings. The bright red may startle predators. Wingspan to 3 $3/4$ inches. Found in wooded areas; it spends the winter as an egg on its host plants of poplar and willow. Look for this moth during August and September.

Formosa Looper *Chrysanympha formosa*

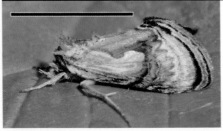

Formosa in Latin means "beautiful," and this moth certainly is. Forewing pattern and coloration is unmistakable; the hind wings are grayish brown. Found in northern woodlands where it lays it eggs on blueberry. Adults fly May to July.

Clearwing Moths
Family Sesiidae

Appearance

Small to moderate in size with wings that either completely or mostly lack scales. The forewings are long and narrow; wasp-like in appearance.

Biology

Day-flying moths commonly on flowers or resting on foliage. They lay eggs on a variety of plants, trees and shrubs where the larvae are borers.

Dogwood Borer   *Synanthedon scitula*

Both wings are clear with brown on the forward edge of the forewing. The legs are yellow with a black band on the hind legs. The Dogwood Borer lays eggs on a variety of deciduous trees and shrubs including dogwood, birch, apple, oak and black cherry. Watch for it June to July.

Plume Moths
Family Pterophoridae

Appearance

Small, slender moths with a wingspan commonly between $2/3$ to $7/8$ inch wide. The forewings are divided into two lobes while the hind wings are divided into three.

Biology

They lay eggs on a variety of plants where the larvae are leaf rollers or borers.

Plume Moth   *Platyptilia species*

Plume moths hold their wings close to together and at a right angles when at rest (looks like a T). The legs are long and spiny. Commonly active June to July.

Scorpionflies
Order Mecoptera

Diversity
There are five families and 83 species in North America. The scorpionflies are moderately common in the North Woods.

Appearance
Adults: Scorpionflies are medium-sized, slender, cylindrical, soft-bodied insects, ranging from 1/8 to 1/2 inch in length. They have a long looking face because of a prolonged beak; their chewing mouthparts are locat-ed at the end of this beak. Scorpionflies have moderate to long slender antennae. They have four long, narrow membranous wings, often with bands or spots; one small group is wingless. The tip of the abdomen of common scorpionfly males is bulbous and held over their back, giving them the appearance of a scorpion. Scorpionflies are typically yellowish or reddish brown, rarely black.

"Hey, why the long face?" This head-on view of a scorpionfly highlights the elongated beak that gives them a long-faced look.

Larvae: Many scorpionfly larvae are caterpillar-like with small prolegs on eight abdominal segments. They have a couple of fleshy spines on the tail end of their abdomen, although a few have spines covering their entire body. Other scorpionfly larvae are grub-like lacking prolegs and spines. Scorpionfly larvae are rarely encountered.

Habitats
Scorpionflies are found in deciduous forests where they are found on low foliage or hanging from stems or the edge of leaves. One small group is associated with snow.

Life Cycle
Scorpionflies are holometabolous insects, using complete metamorphosis to develop. They typically have complex mating rituals where the males offer females food (dead insects) or secrete spittle to entice them to mate. Males lacking such a gift may try to forcefully mate with females. They lay eggs in soil, rotting wood, or moss where the larvae live. Larvae take about a month to mature. Eventually they pupate in the soil. There is typically one generation a year.

Food

Both adult and immature scorpionflies feed on dead insects; they may also feed on decaying animal matter. Some scorpionflies are predacious on other insects while a few feed on moss.

Don't confuse them with...

...wasps. You can distinguish between them as wasps lack a prolonged beak and they never have a scorpion-like abdomen. You may also confuse scorpionflies with true flies, especially crane flies, however true flies also lack a prolonged peak and only have two wings.

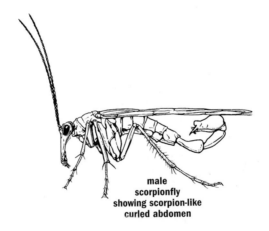

**male
scorpionfly
showing scorpion-like
curled abdomen**

Common Scorpionflies
Family Panorpidae

Appearance

Moderate sized scorpionflies about ⅜ inch in length. They are typically yellowish brown and black bands or spots on their wings. The tip of the abdomen of males is enlarged and usually held over their back giving them the appearance of a scorpion; despite their appearance, they are harmless to people.

Biology

Common scorpionflies are found in deciduous forests and forest edges where they are found on the leaves of low lying shrubs or herbaceous plants. They feed primarily on dead insects, although they have even been known to steal insects from spider webs. Scorpionflies are wary and are often difficult to approach closely. They are common June and July, although can be seen as early as May or later in August.

Scorpionfly *Panorpa species*

Scorpionflies are interesting creatures. Courtship involves the male offering the female a gift, often a dead insect (Every woman's dream!). The common name comes from the harmless curled tip of the male's abdomen that resembles a scorpion prepared to strike (see bottom photo). The red protuberance on the thorax of the female in the top photo is actually a red mite. The scorpionfly is not a true fly; If it was a true fly in the order Diptera, its common name would be written as two words—"scorpion fly." In wooded areas June through July.

Snow Scorpionflies
Family Boreidae

Appearance
Small, 1/8 inch long insects that are dark brown or black. Females are wingless while males have short, slender, hard wings they use when mating.

Biology
Snow scorpionflies are active on the snow or moss during the winter, especially late winter or early spring as snow is melting. They can be active down to 21 degrees F. The larvae develop on moss. Both adults and larvae feed on moss. Although they can not fly, if they feel threatened, snow scorpionflies can jump straight up and land with their legs folded to try to resemble a bit of dirt.

Snow Scorpionfly · *Boreus brumalis*

Look on top of the snow on warmer winter days for this interesting critter. They feed on mosses and liverworts. Short wings are modified into sharp points in males that they use to grasp the female during mating. Females have no apparent wings.

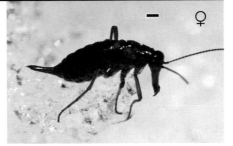

True Flies
Order Diptera

Diversity

There are 105 families and over 19,000 species in North America, making this group one of the largest insect orders. The true flies are very common in the North Woods.

Appearance

Adults: Most true flies are small to medium-sized $^1/_{16}$ to $^1/_2$ inch long, although some species can measure over an inch in size. They are generally soft-bodied ranging from slender to robust. They are usually dark-colored, although some are black and yellow, green, and some are even metallic green or blue. True flies, unlike most insects, have just two thin, membranous wings while the second pair of wings are reduced to a pair of small knob-like organs called halteres. They have sucking mouthparts which vary considerably, e.g. sponging/lapping, piercing, and slashing. True flies typically have short antennae.

Larvae: True fly larvae, often referred to as maggots, are worm-like, legless, and often slender. They often lack a conspicuous head, although some species possess a well developed, prominent head. The mouthparts are variable, ranging from conspicuous mandibles to mouthparts reduced to rasping mouth hooks.

Habitats

True flies are found in essentially all habitats. Adults are commonly found on flowers and foliage. The larvae are found in all types of water, decaying plant and animal matter, as well as in living plants, such as leaves, stems, fruits and roots where they feed.

Life Cycle

True flies are holometabolous insects, using complete metamorphosis to develop. Individual true flies are generally short-lived. Eggs are inconspicuous and are laid close to a food source. Many species construct a protective covering around the pupa known as a puparium (pl. puparia). The puparium often consists of the last shed larval "skin," darkened and hardened into a capsule-like envelope. The pupae of many aquatic species can swim.

Food

Adult true flies feed on a variety of liquids including nectar, blood, sap, and honeydew as well as semi-liquid material, such as feces. Some true flies are predaceous on other insects. Blood feeders typically are able to find a blood meal through a combination of carbon dioxide, warmth, moisture, and chemical smells the hosts give off.

Don't confuse them with...

...bees and wasps. You can distinguish between them because bees and wasps have two pair of wings, chewing mouthparts, and often have longer antennae. It is also possible to confuse true flies with lacewings and other nerve-winged insects which also have four wings, chewing mouthparts, and moderately long antennae.

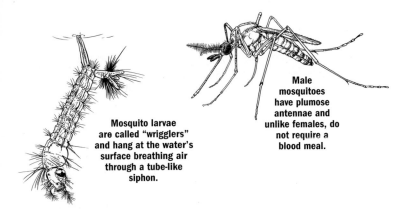

Mosquito larvae are called "wrigglers" and hang at the water's surface breathing air through a tube-like siphon.

Male mosquitoes have plumose antennae and unlike females, do not require a blood meal.

Crane Flies
Family Tipulidae

Appearance

Many folks mistakenly refer to these slender flies with long legs as "giant mosquitoes." They range in size from 3/8 to 1 1/2 inches long. They have brown or gray bodies with wings that are often banded. Crane flies have a V-shaped groove on their thorax.

Some crane flies hang vertically.

Biology

Crane flies are usually associated with moist, damp environments with an abundance of vegetation, especially wooded areas near sources of moisture. They are typically found resting in shaded areas on foliage close to the ground. Despite their appearance to large mosquitoes, crane flies do not bite. They usually live for only a few days and typically don't feed. Crane flies are common spring and summer.

Crane Fly *Epiphragma fasciapenne*

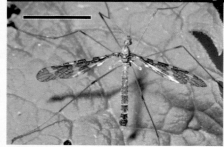

Intricately patterned wings are banded with brown and cream. Found in moist woodlands on the leaf litter or on low foliage. May and June.

Crane Fly *Gnophomyia tristissima*

Gnophomyia tristissima is a small all black species. Also note the white-yellow halteres; these are structures that evolved from the hind pair of wings. Its larvae develop inside cut or fallen hardwood logs that are rotting. Can be common in suitable areas. Watch for this crane fly during July and August.

Giant Eastern Crane Fly *Pedicia albivitta*

Adults of this huge species are often found near wooded ponds and sluggish creeks. Though the body length is impressive enough (1 1/2 inches; note size bar), wingspan is over two inches and legspan over three inches! Attracted to artificial light (hence the photo inside a cabin).

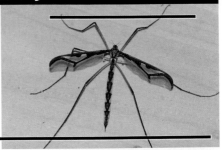

legspan ●━━━━━━━━━━━━━━━

Giant Crane Fly *Tipula abdominalis*

This huge crane fly has a dark brown or black and gray thorax and dark colored abdomen with yellow running down the upper surface. It has clear wings with several small smoky brown spots. This crane fly is common July and August.

Crane Fly *Erioptera chlorophylla*

Tiny and pale green. Larvae develop in moist or saturated soils near shorelines. Look for them in low vegetation near water. This specimen was photographed clinging to an alder leaf near the quiet waters above a rapids in early July.

Wingless Crane Fly *Chionea valga*

Chionea valga is found throughout the winter on snow where it can survive temperatures as low as minus 25 degrees F. May live two months. Wingless and spider-like in appearance. Found in deciduous and evergreen woodlands, especially around rocky sites where it is suspected to spend much of its life cycle in rodent burrows.

Phantom Crane Flies
Family Ptychopteridae

Appearance

Slender flies with long legs that resemble crane flies, they are about 1/4 to 1/2 inch long. They are dark colored, sometimes with white bands on their legs. Some species have banded wings.

Biology

Phantom crane flies are found in wooded areas and near marshes and other damp sites. They are not particularly good flyers and are commonly carried by the wind. Look for phantom crane flies during spring and summer.

Phantom Crane Fly *Bittacomorpha clavipes*

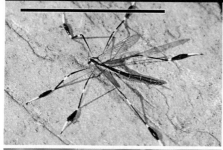

Seeing one of these insects in flight will surely catch your attention; They almost float through the air, banded legs outstretched, "swollen ankles" catching the breeze. Legs may span more than an inch. It is associated with swampy areas and is found from May through September.

Winter Crane Flies
Family Trichoceridae

Appearance
Small to medium, 1/5 to 2/5 inch long slender insects. Winter crane flies are very similar to crane flies but have ocelli, i.e. simple eyes, on top of their head which crane flies lack (you need magnification to see ocelli).

Biology
Winter crane flies can be found during late winter and early spring walking on snow, often congregated in large numbers. Adults don't feed while the larvae feed on decaying plant material.

Winter Crane Fly *Trichocera species*

Mild days in early winter or late winter is when you may spy a winter crane fly of genus *Trichocera*. And like the photo shows, they will be on top of the snow.

Black Flies
Family Simulidae

Appearance

Small, stout flies from $\frac{1}{16}$ to $\frac{1}{4}$ inch long. They are black, dark brown, or grayish with short legs and broad wings. Black flies have a humpbacked appearance.

Biology

Black flies are particularly associated with rivers, streams and other types of moving water, especially in wooded areas. Female black flies bite vertebrate animals, including humans, while males feed on nectar. Fortunately black flies are not known to transmit disease to people in the North Woods. Black flies are particularly common during spring and early summer but can also be found throughout the summer.

Black Flies attraction to blue is a well known fact amongst wilderness travelers. This photo was taken in June in Minnesota's Boundary Waters Canoe Area.

Black Fly *Simulium species*

Anyone who's travelled the North Woods by foot or by canoe in June has endured the vicious attacks of female black flies. They are tiny, ranging from $\frac{1}{16}$ to $\frac{1}{8}$ inch long and are black, dark brown to gray. Eggs are laid on leaves or stones in or near the edges of moving water. Larva develop in these fast moving and clean rivers.

Some species, especially *S. venustum*, are vicious biters of people. Black flies are common from spring through early summer.

Mosquitoes
Family Culicidae

Appearance

Slender, small flies with long legs that range from 1/8 to 5/16 inch long. They have scales on their wings and conspicuous long mouthparts. Mosquitoes are usually colored brown or gray.

Male mosquitoes have feathery antennae and do not bite.

Biology

Mosquitoes are particularly common around sources of standing water, like ponds and marshes, although they can be found essentially anywhere in the North Woods. Peak activity occurs at dusk and dawn. Female mosquitoes feed on blood of a variety of vertebrate animals, including humans, while males feed on flower nectar. Mosquitoes are present spring and summer, although they are generally less common during dry weather. Some mosquito species vector disease to humans, such as West Nile Virus.

Females require a blood meal (be it human or otherwise) to produce eggs.

Mosquito   *Aedes vexans*

This is one of our most common biting species, *Aedes vexans*. Its legs are banded black and white. Most *Aedes* mosquitoes species are brownish or grayish bodies with legs that are banded black and white or are just black. They overwinter as eggs and are typically associated with marshes and other semipermanent water. They are present from May until September.

March Flies
Family Bibionidae

Appearance

Small to medium flies, from ¼ to ½ inch long. March flies are generally dark, sometimes with red and yellow, and are hairy or bristly. They have a large, bulging thorax and a generally flattened abdomen. Males have eyes where the facets in the upper two-thirds are larger than those in the lower third.

Biology

March flies are common around flowers in fields where decaying organic matter is common, such as decaying leaves, grass roots, and manure. Some species can occur in large mating swarms. Pairs have a tendency to remain coupled for hours, even days, due to the male's strong claspers. March flies are common in spring and early summer.

March Fly *Bibio species*

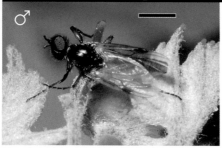

Though not typically seen as early as March in the North Woods, this group is common late April to early June. They are shiny black with clear wings that have yellowish brown veins and a spot on the forward edge of each wing. They lay eggs in the soil where the larvae live during summer. Overwinter as pupae.

Dark-winged Fungus Gnats
Family Sciaridae

Appearance

Small, most species are between ¹⁄₁₆ to ⅛ inch long. Dark-winged fungus gnats are slender, dark-colored flies with moderate-length antennae.

Biology

Dark-winged fungus gnats are associated with damp, shady conditions, especially decaying wood and leaf litter, where the larvae feed on fungi. Adults can also be found visiting flowers. Some species are found indoors and are especially associated with over-watered houseplants or other conditions where fungi is growing.

Dark-winged Fungus Gnat *Family Sciaridae*

Very small insects. Some species with long mouthparts can be very common on blooming flowers. This group was photographed on an Ox-eye Daisy in mid July.

Midges
Family Chironomidae

Appearance

Small to moderate, delicate mosquito-like flies, ranging in size from $1/16$ to $3/8$ inch long with moderate sized legs. The first pair is usually the longest and is held up while at rest. Midges lack scales on their wings and functioning mouthparts. Males have feather-like antennae. Midges are often gray, brown, or green.

Biology

Midges are weak flyers and are found near sources of water, typically resting on low foliage. Despite their resemblance to mosquitoes, they do not bite people. In fact adult midges do not feed and are short lived. Midges can occur in very large mating swarms, especially in the evening. You can see midges throughout the year but they are particularly common during spring.

Male midges have feathery antennae.

Midges can be seen any time of the year—even on top of the snow in winter.

Horse Flies & Deer Flies
Family Tabanidae

Appearance

Medium to large sized, stout insects measuring from ¼ to one inch long. They have very large eyes which are often brightly patterned iridescent green, turquoise or purple (see photos). The eyes of the males touch while are separate in the females. Horse flies and deer flies range in color from black to brown to yellow.

Deer Fly eyes can be iridescent blue, green or red.

Biology

The fearsome slashing-sucking mouthparts of a horse fly.

Horse flies and deer flies are found in woodlands and open areas along the edges of wooded areas. The females use slashing-sucking mouthparts to feed on the blood of mammals, including humans, as well as birds while males feed on nectar and pollen. Horse flies and deer flies are common throughout the summer.

Deer Fly *Chrysops species*

Is there a more annoying insect in the North Woods? Maybe mosquitoes, black flies or horse flies could vie for the title, but when a persistent deer fly is hovering around your head, they win hands down. Of course it is a female just doing her job and looking for a blood meal. Note the iridescent eyes; Their eyes are typically have a multicolored pattern. Deer flies range from ¼ to ³/₈ inch long and have some type of banding on their wings. Deer flies are common from June to August.

Horse Fly   *Hybomitra lasiophthalma*

Spots of sunlight in dense woods is where you may see a hovering *Hybomitra* horse fly. Males aggressively dart at other males who are vying for the same female (or they may be guarding terrestrial larvae). On quiet mornings, the sound of many hovering males (especially along shrubby ditches) can be quite loud.

Horse Fly   *Atylotus bicolor*

The first thing you may notice about this horse fly is its yellow-green eyes; not a common trait in the Tabanidae. Yellowish abdomen and top of thorax. White face. This specimen was photographed in Leatherleaf (*Chamaedaphne calyculata*) along a pool in an open stunted Black Spruce bog.

Horse Fly   *Tabanus species*

If your ankles are exposed while canoeing, you are just simply horse fly bait. Females can painfully bite as they seek a blood meal. Fortunately, they are much slower than deer flies. Horse flies may reach an inch long. They are black or brown, typically with stripes on their abdomens. Eyes are either a solid color or have stripes. Late June to August.

Black Horse Fly   *Tabanus atratus*

Black Horse Flies are large and striking insects. We can tell this is a harmless male as the large eyes are joined and not separated as in females. Only females need vertebrate blood. Wings and eyes are solid black. They are found from June to August.

Snipe Flies
Family Rhagionidae

Appearance

Medium sized flies measuring ³/₁₆ to ¹/₄ with a fairly hairless body. They have a somewhat round head with a relatively long, tapering abdomen and long legs. They are typically brownish or grayish and often have spots on their wings.

Biology

Snipe flies live in wooded areas, especially near moist sites where they are common on foliage. Snipe flies are usually predaceous and are common from May to July.

Snipe Fly   *Chrysopilus quadratus*

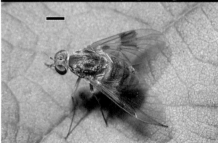

This snipe fly is dark brown with smoky brown patches on its wings. Larvae in soil or rotting wood. Look for it during June and July.

Snipe Fly   *Rhagio mystaceous*

Note the dark bands on its abdomen. This common snipe fly is light brown with pale dark stripes on its thorax and small brown markings on its wings. Males seem to set up territories on large horizontal leaves along woodland paths. Sometimes perch head-down on tree trunks. *Rhagio mystaceous* is common from May to July.

Golden-backed Snipe Fly *Chrysopilus thoracicus*

A striking species with smoky black wings. The similar *C. ornatus* has clear wings and a more distinctly banded abdomen. Larvae in soil or rotting wood.

Soldier Flies
Family Stratiomyidae

Appearance
Medium sized flies, ⅛ to ⅗ inch long. Soldier flies are variously colored, including green, yellow, black, and blue often with a patterned abdomen. The abdomen is often flat and broad. Many mimic wasps

Biology
Soldier flies are found in a variety of habitats including forests, meadows, and near ponds, lakes, or moist areas. They visit flowers, such, feeding on nectar and pollen. Larvae occur in a variety of situations; some are aquatic, some are associated with decaying organic material, others occur under bark, and other habitats. Soldier flies are commonly encountered from May through August.

Soldier Fly *Odontomyia cincta*

Search for bright green soldier flies sitting quietly on pondside flowers and leaves in early summer. Larvae are aquatic and feed on algae. Look for these soldier flies from May to July.

Robber Flies
Family Asilidae

Appearance

Medium to large flies, measuring between 3/8 to well over an inch in length. They may be slender and smooth bodied or stout, hairy and bumble bee-like. Robber flies possess large, bulging eyes creating a hollowed out space between them at the top. Their face appears bearded and they have a short, stout beak-like mouthparts. Robber flies have long, strong legs. Color varies.

If robber flies were the size of dogs we'd all be in trouble! This *Laphria* species has taken a damselfly.

Biology

Robber flies live in a variety of habitats depending on the species. They are predacious on many types of insects. Robber flies are strong flyers, and usually capture prey on the wing. It is not unusual for them to capture insects larger than themselves. Some have a flattened knife-like beak which allows them to penetrate between the wing covers and joints of the exoskeleton of beetles. Common spring and summer.

Robber Fly   *Proctacanthus rufus*

A real beach-goer, *Proctacanthus rufus* is partial to beaches and dunes along big lakes and rivers. This monster was photographed hunting in the sand dunes along Lake Superior in Duluth, Minnesota. You can get an idea of their size by the bottom photo where this female has captured a large bumble bee (*Bombus ternarius*). Photo taken in late July.

Milbert's Robber Fly *Proctacanthus milbertii*

Possibly the most common large robber fly in the North Woods. Prefers hunting in open dry areas such as dunes, beaches and savannahs. To give you an idea of how large these flies are, note the size of the adult grasshopper this *Proctocanthus milbertii* has seized.

Robber Fly *Machimus notatus*

Maybe our most common woodland robber fly species. *Machimus* robber flies are brownish or grayish. They feed on a variety prey including moths, spittlebugs, blow flies and mosquitoes. Look for them June to August.

Robber Fly *Neoitamus orphne*

Distinctly pointed, the females abdomen is used to place eggs in flowers or leaves. This robber fly species has a gray thorax with black markings, a black abdomen with gray bands, and orange and black legs. It occurs June and July.

Three-banded Robber Fly *Stichopogon trifasciatus*

Beaches of lakes and rivers are a favored habitats for this common robber fly. It has a gray head, thorax (the dorsum often appears dark gray) and legs. Look for the distinct banding on the abdomen; brown with three white bands (or white with dark bands depending on your perspective). July to August.

Robber Fly *Laphria canis complex*

Laphria canis is a complex of possibly several species that we'll treat as one here. They are smaller and less hairy than most North Woods *Laphria*, with only sparse hairs on the thorax. Hunt in sun-dappled woodlands. Note the large genital bulb at the tip of the abdomen. Late June and July.

Robber Fly *Laphria cinerea*

This robber has captured a click beetle (*Ampedus apicatus*) on an old fallen log. Note the sparse scutellum hairs, the pale hair tuft in front of the wings and that the pile on the sixth abdominal segment is pale yellow. This early July photo represents the second Minnesota sight record. Rare (or overlooked?). Logs and stumps in cut pine woods.

Robber Fly *Laphria flavicollis*

Though difficult to see in this photo, the abdomen is all black. Extremely fast and regularly preys on honey bees; this specimen is devouring a damselfly. Launches attacks from sunlit leaves in wooded areas. Open woods throughout the eastern U.S. Early season robber; found June to mid July.

Robber Fly *Laphria huron*

A rather rare (or overlooked?) robber fly of the Great Lakes and New England. This photo is one of only two live specimens on the internet (the other from Mike Reese in Wisconsin). Femur and tibiae of front and middle legs covered with long yellow hairs. Thorax has yellow hairs. Flies in early to mid summer.

Robber Fly *Laphria janus*

Reddish abdomen hairs contrasting with the yellow thoracic hairs are an easy field mark in identifying this species. Also note the thick golden beard. Yellow thoracic hairs not spread over entire thorax so some black shows through. Great Lakes and northeastern U.S. and Canada. Late May to early August.

Robber Fly *Laphria posticata*

Attractive species. Look for the yellow pile on abdominal segments 4 and 5 (segments 6 and 7 are all black). Male's beard entirely yellow. Reddish-gold thoracic hairs. Larvae have been collected from White Pine stumps. Found from New England to Minnesota and across northern Canada to Alaska. June through August.

Robber Fly *Laphria sacrator*

A very fuzzy northern species with long and dense yellow hairs on the thorax and first three segments of the abdomen; rear half of abdomen black. Naturalist Mike Reese points out that the fine red hairs on the front legs is very visible with binoculars. Maybe the most believable bumble bee mimic of all the *Laphria*. Flies June through July.

Robber Fly *Laphria sericea / aktis complex*

The two species, *L. sericea* and *L. aktis*, are not separable in the field so are lumped together here. Golden-red hairs cover the abdomen and top of the thorax. A whitish beard and black hairs above the eyes. Look for them in dry oak woods or moist woods near water. Early June through July.

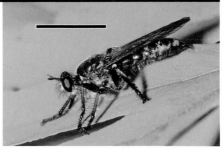

Bee Flies
Family Bombylidae

Appearance

Small to moderate, stout flies from $1/10$ to $5/8$ inch long. They are hairy and hold their wings straight out when at rest. The wings are often patterned. They range in color from black to brown, some with a dense mat of yellow hairs, others with white hairs which are often in bands. They have long, slender mouthparts.

Biology

Bee flies are commonly found in sunny areas particularly on flowers where they feed on nectar. They are good flyers and can hover and dart off suddenly. They generally lay eggs in the nests of ground-nesting solitary wasps and bees and grasshopper eggs where their larvae are ectoparasites. Look for bee flies spring and summer.

Greater Bee Fly *Bombylius major*

Like this photo shows, Greater Bee Flies can often be seen nectaring at spring/early summer wildflowers like this Wild Strawberry blossom. They also hover in sunny patches in woods. Wings with dark leading edge. Larvae parasitize the larvae of solitary bees such as andrenid bees (*Andrena* species). June and July.

Pygmy Bee Fly *Bombylius pygmaeus*

This attractive smaller species was photographed minutes after the above species. It also is an early season bee fly of northern woods. White "belt" around its middle and white at front of thorax. Spots on wings. Note the extremely long beak. Parasitoid of solitary bees. June and July.

Bee Fly   *Villa lateralis*

A variable eastern species with several recognizable forms. The larvae are parasitic on moth caterpillars. Wide ranging; found from Canada south to Panama. Late June to September.

Bee Fly   *Exoprosopa fascipennis*

An attractive and colorful bee fly. Larvae are parasitic on other parasites of soil-dwelling insect larvae (Say that ten times fast!). The female actually hovers above a likely burrow of a solitary wasp and literally shoots her eggs into the hole. Hopefully her larvae will develop as ectoparasites on the wasp larvae. July to September.

Sinuous Bee Fly   *Hemipenthes sinuosa.*

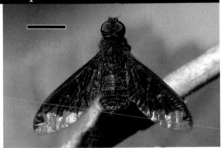

Interestingly, the larva of this species is parasitic on other larval parasites who are already inside their caterpillar host! This bee fly has a black body and mostly black wings. It has a globular-shaped head. Commonly found on composite flowers during May to August.

Bee Fly   *Poecilanthrax alcyon*

A large bee fly with a marbled pattern on the wings. *Poecilanthrax alcyon* larvae are parasitic on cutworms and armyworms in the soil. July and August.

Bee Fly   *Poecilognathus sulphureus*

This bee fly is slightly hump-backed. It has a yellow body with red to orange markings and has clear wings. It is commonly seen on composite flowers from July to September.

Hunch-backed Fly   *Lepidophora lutea / L. lepidocera*

I've heard of the Hunchback of Notre Dame, but the Hunchback of the North Woods? This fly has a decidedly humped back. Both species of *Lepidophora* (*L. lutea* and *L. lepidocera*) develop inside the nests of solitary wasps as keptoparasites or parasites. July and August.

Long-legged Flies
Family Dolichopodidae

Appearance

Small to moderate sized flies ranging ¹/₁₆ to ¹/₄ inch long. They are relatively slender with long legs. Long-legged flies are typically iridescent green, blue, or copper. Some males have conspicuous tufts of scales on their legs.

Biology

Long-legged flies are found in many types of habitats including woodland, prairies, meadows, especially when they are close to swamps and streams. They are typically found on foliage where they make short, darting movements. These flies are predaceous on small-sized insects. Long-legged flies are common from June through August.

Long-legged Fly *Condylostylus species*

When watching these long-legged flies walk around on vegetation, they almost seem to change color—from iridescent green to gold to coppery. Though tiny, they walk about on proportionately very long legs (hence, the common name). The wings are usually clear, although some species have smokey or banded wings. They are common in meadows and woodlands, especially near marshy or swampy areas. They are common June through August.

Long-legged Fly *Dolichopus remipes*

The photo shows the micro-habitat of this iridescent green species quite well—floating aquatic vegetation is the best place to see *Dolichopus*. The back legs of males are fringed with long hairs. This long-legged fly is found near lakes, including on water plants, from May through September.

Long-legged Fly *Hydrophorus species*

These long-legged flies can walk on water. They search out living or dead prey on the water's surface. You could almost be fooled into mistaking them for little water striders by the way they move across the surface of stagnant puddles—until you get a closer look.

Flower Flies
Family Syrphidae

Appearance

Slender to robust flies, commonly ranging in length from 3/8 to 3/4 inch long. They are often black and yellow striped, sometimes black with orange or brown. Most are smooth-bodied, although some are fuzzy. Flower flies mimic bees or wasps.

Biology

Flower flies are very common in many different habitats and are frequently seen on flowers and foliage. They commonly hover around plants and can abruptly dart off in a different direction. After they land, their abdomens commonly bob up and down. Despite their menacing appearance, flower flies are harmless to people. The larvae of some species feed on aphids while others develop in aquatic environments and feed on organic debris. The well known "rat-tailed maggot" is the aquatic larva of the Drone Fly; its long breathing tube gives the larvae its common name.

Flower Fly *Spilomyia fusca*

An obvious and very good Bald-faced Hornet mimic. It sometimes pays to look dangerous. Also note the wonderfully patterned eyes. Flies June to September.

Flower Fly *Parhelophilus rex*

When the Bullhead Lilies (*Nuphar luteum*) bloom in June to July, watch for this feisty species. They are likely a major pollinator of this plant. This specimen was photographed in the Boundary Waters of Minnesota in late June. It constantly battled with other adults over individual Bullhead Lilies.

Drone Fly *Eristalis tenax*

Fuzzier than many flower flies, the Drone Fly is a pretty good honey bee mimic. It is very common in spring and fall. The eggs laid in organically polluted water (like mud puddles in cow pastures) develop into aquatic larvae called "rat-tailed maggots," named for their retractable breathing tube. May to September.

Flower Fly *Eristalis dimidiata*

Flies from late spring until late fall—late April to October—and is one of the first syrphids out and about.

Flower Fly *Helophilus species*

This robust flower fly species is dark brown to black thorax with four yellow stripes and a dark brown to black abdomen with yellow bands. Look for this flower fly from July to September.

Flower Fly *Sericomyia militaris*

Maybe not as good a Bald-faced Hornet mimic as *Spilomyia fusca*, but it fooled the photographer. The aquatic larvae have long breathing tubes. Late May to October.

Common Oblique Syrphid *Allograpta obliqua*

Expert flyers that can effortlessly hover. Often seen nectaring at flowers (like this specimen on an Ox-eye Daisy) or hovering near aphid colonies where they feed on honeydew exuded by the aphids, and where they lay eggs. Larvae develop in these colonies, becoming slug-like predators of the aphids. Common in July.

Flower Fly *Syrphus or Epistrophe species*

There are several genera of syrphids that look remarkably similar. Many *Syrphus* females visit flowers apparently to feed on pollen instead of nectar; they seem to prefer to get their "sugar fix" from the honeydew of aphids. Larvae are predatory, often on aphids.

Flower Fly *Toxomerus geminatus*

Spend any time in a domestic flower garden or patch of wildflowers in late summer and you will likely see dozens of *Toxomerus* individuals of several species. Immediately noticeable is their flattened abdomen and hovering ability. Larvae feed on aphids.

Flower Fly *Toxomerus marginatus*

This species is very similar to *T. geminatus* but note the yellow margin (hence *marginatus*) to the abdomen (just visible in the photo). They have an olive brown thorax with yellow along the edges and a flattened abdomen with an intricate pattern of yellow and olive brown. Watch for this flower fly from July to September.

Flower Fly *Sphaerophoria species*

This flower fly has a black and yellow thorax and a slender black and yellow striped abdomen. Shiny gold on the thorax. Wings can reflect a multicolored sheen when seen in the right light (not unique to this genus). Species can show much variation in markings (note specimen with reddish-abdomen). Larvae are slug-like predators of aphids. It is common from July to September.

Dung Flies
Family Scathophagidae

Appearance

Small to moderate sized flies, 1/8 to 1/2 inch long moderately slender bodies. They are often yellowish and hairy, although some species are dark-colored.

Biology

Most dung flies are associated with fresh dung, the food of the larvae. Other species are associated with plants, either boring into stems or as leafminers. Adults prey on smaller insects.

Golden Dung Fly *Scathophaga stercoraria*

The world of the Golden Dung Fly revolves around cow poop. They breed in it, the female lays her eggs in it and the males defend it as precious territory. It is an attractive fly with a not so attractive home. Also called Pilose Yellow Dung Fly. May also be found on spring flowers including Bloodroot. April to June and August to September.

Muscid Flies
Family Muscidae

Appearance

Small to medium sized, moderate to robust-bodied flies, ranging in length from ⅛ to ½ inch long. They are blackish, brownish, or grayish, although some are yellow or metallic green or blue. They are more or less conspicuously bristled.

Biology

Muscid flies are found in many habitats. They are associated with decaying organic matter, including dung, although some species feed on blood from mammals (both females and males bite) while others are predaceous on insects. Muscid flies are found spring and summer.

Muscid Fly *Mesembrina species*

Yellow wing bases and brick red eyes make this shiny black species stand out. It lays its eggs in dung, especially in hardwood forests. Look for this muscid fly in July and August.

House Fly *Musca domestica*

Though not only found in houses, the House Fly can pass diseases on to humans. It has a dull gray body with four dark stripes on the thorax, a black or grayish abdomen highlighted with yellowish brown. It lays eggs in manure, decaying vegetation and garbage. They are present spring and summer and are particularly numerous during warm weather.

Muscid Fly *Neomyia cornicina*

Dung piles would be a good place to start your search for this species as this is where it lays its eggs. This muscid fly has an iridescent green or blue-green thorax and abdomen. It is present from June to September.

Stable Fly *Stomoxys calcitrans*

"Ankle-biter" is an appropriate name for this annoying species (annoying for its human and mammalian victims). Long, needle-like mouthparts are used for biting. It lays eggs in decaying plant material, especially along lakes shores and pastures. Note grayish thorax with four black stripes. July to September.

Root-maggot Flies Family Anthomyiidae

Appearance

Small to medium sized flies that are blackish, grayish, brownish with black bristles. They are similar to muscid flies but are usually more slender.

Biology

Commonly on foliage and are relatively slow to fly off when approached by people. Many are reported to be predacious. Common May into August.

Root-maggot Fly *Hylemya alcathoe*

Males are known to perch in large numbers on low-lying herbaceous plants in order to mate with females that fly by. This fly has a brownish gray thorax and abdomen with brown and black legs. It is common in woodlands and adjacent areas in May and June.

Blow Flies
Family Calliphoridae

Appearance
Small to medium sized, moderate-bodied flies, measuring between 1/4 to 5/8 inch long. Many blow flies are metallic green or blue, although some species are blackish. Bristles are more or less conspicuous.

Blow flies are often seen on carcasses.

Biology
Blow flies are often associated with decaying organic matter, particularly carcasses and other sources of rotting meat and feces. In fact, they can figure prominently in forensic entomology., aiding in determining time of death. It is also common to find them on flowers. Blow flies are common spring and summer.

Common Green Bottle Fly *Phaenicia sericata*

What's a nice guy like you doing in a place like this? This beautiful iridescent green fly can often be found on roadkill. In fact, this blow fly is one of the first insects to discover a freshly killed carcass. It is iridescent green, green-blue or coppery. It is also commonly found on excrement. Common from May to September.

Cluster Fly *Pollenia rudis*

This transplant from Europe, specializes in parasitizing earthworms, producing two or three generations a year. It is black with short, yellow hairs on the sides of the thorax. Its wings overlap when at rest. Cluster flies can be found spring, summer and fall (as well as winter inside homes).

Flesh Flies
Family Sarcophagidae

Appearance

Small to medium usually moderate to robust-bodied flies, measuring in size from $1/16$ to $1/2$ inch long with bristles on their body. Flesh flies are typically black or gray (never metallic) usually with dark colored stripes on the thorax.

Biology

Flesh flies are found in many habitats and are commonly associated with dead animals. The larvae of some species eat other insects, stealing the paralyzed prey from wasps. Unlike most insects, female flesh flies lay live young. They are found from spring to summer.

Friendly Fly *Sarcophaga aldrichi*

"Friendly" is a matter of opinion; This large fly gets this happy common name from its habit of landing on people and being difficult to shoo away. And they can swarm in tremendously large numbers when forest tent caterpillars (Latin) are common. You see, the Friendly Fly is a forest tent caterpillar parasite, laying its eggs on the unfortunate moth caterpillars. But contrary to popular belief, they do not bite. Friendly Flies have a blue-gray and black striped thorax and a blue-gray and black checked abdomen. They are common from June to early August.

Parasitic Flies
Family Tachinidae

Appearance

Medium sized, generally stocky flies, typically ranging from 1/8 to 3/4 inch long. They are conspicuously bristly and possess an enlarged postscutellum (a swelling on the posterior area of the thorax). Most parasitic flies are dark colored, sometime with white, some resemble bees or wasps and most are difficult to distinguish from muscid flies and root-maggot flies.

Biology

Parasitic flies (also known as tachinid flies) are common in many habitats and are often found visiting flowers. They commonly parasitize other insects, typically immature moth, butterflies, sawflies, beetles, true bugs and grasshoppers. Females have several strategies for delivering their young to hosts. They can lay eggs on or in hosts, lay eggs nearby and allow the maggots to hatch and find hosts, or lay eggs, which are particularly small, on leaves which are consumed by the hosts. Parasitic flies are found spring and summer.

Parasitic Fly *Ptilodexia species*

Ptilodexia flies parasitize a variety of beetles, especially June beetles (family Scarabaeidae) and some long-horned beetles (family Cerambycidae). These parasitic flies typically have a gray and black thorax and abdomen, although there are a few species with reddish brown areas on the sides of the abdomen. They are common July and August when they are often found on asters (photo) and goldenrods (*Solidago* spp.).

Parasitic Fly *Archytas apicifer*

The silvery white face and bristly black abdomen help to identify *Archytas* flies. They parasitize moth caterpillars, such as forest tent caterpillars and are found on a variety of flowers including Queen Anne's Lace, mint and goldenrod during July and August.

Parasitic Fly *Peleteria species*

Caterpillars better watch out— this genera specializes in seeking them out to lay its eggs on. Very bristly species with burnt orange abdomen marked with black. July and August.

Parasitic Fly *Cylindromyia species*

Certainly a wasp mimic with its long slender abdomen marked with red. *Cylindromyia* parasitizes stink bugs (family Pentatomidae). Other members of the subfamily Phasiinae attack adult and larval beetles. June and July.

Fruit Flies
Family Tephritidae

Appearance

Small to medium sized flies, measuring $1/8$ to $3/8$ inch long. They wings are often ornately banded or spotted. Fruit flies are variously colored including brown. They have a small, tapered abdomen with females possessing a conspicuous ovipositor.

Biology

Fruit flies are found in a variety of habitats where they lay eggs on many different plant parts and fruits. When found on walking on surfaces, fruit flies often rhythmically move their wings slowly up and down. It is thought that distinctly patterned wings play a role in courtship rituals. Fruit flies are common from May to September.

Festive Fruit Fly *Euaresta festiva*

The colors and markings of this fruit fly certainly are festive, with iridescent apple green eyes, black marked wings and a tan head, thorax and abdomen tipped with black. It is associated with Giant Ragweed (*Ambrosia trifida*). Look for this fruit fly from July to September.

Fruit Fly *Paroxyna albiceps*

This attractive species develops on asters so is more common later in the summer and into September. Its whitish body and head is reflected in its specific epithet *albiceps*, which, in Latin means "white head."

Apple Maggot *Rhagoletis pomonella*

A sometimes serious pest of cultivated apples (It lays its eggs on apples), the Apple Maggot is also found on Hawthorn and other fruits in the wild. In fact the Latin root of its specific epithet *pomonella* refers to apples. Beautifully marked with a white-striped black abdomen, a white spot on its thorax and characteristic black banding on its wings. Present from July into September.

Sunflower Maggot Fly *Strauzia species*

There are several similar *Strauzia* species that lay their eggs in developing plants of the composite family. The Sunflower Maggot Fly female has an abdomen modified to lay eggs; it is hard and very pointed and used to place eggs in the sunflower stem. Larvae feed on stem tissue. Summer.

Goldenrod Gall Fly *Eurosta solidaginis*

We've all seen the gall on goldenrod stems, but few of us have seen the fly that is the cause. The Goldenrod Gall Fly is brownish-yellow with dark zigzags on its wings. It lays its eggs in the stem of *Solidago* goldenrods and the plant responds by growing around the eggs. Downy Woodpeckers and Black-capped Chickadees chisel in to get at the larvae. Adults April to May.

Picture-winged Flies
Family Ulidiidae

Appearance
Small flies, about ⅙ to ⅜ inch long. They typically have metallic colored bodies and wings marked with black, brown, or yellow.

Biology
Picture-winged flies are usually found in moist areas and can become quite numerous in a given area. The larvae feed on decaying plant matter. You can find picture-winged flies from May to August.

Black Onion Fly *Tritoxa flexa*

This picture-winged fly has boldly patterned wings that make this small species quite visible. Often associated with cultivated garlic (a close relative of the onion).

Signal Flies
Family Platystomatidae

Appearance
Colorful and tiny flies that hold their wings outstretched. The wings are constantly in motion, as if signaling, hence the family name.

Biology
Mostly found in fields, some in woodlands. Larvae of *Rivellia* species develop inside the root nodules in legumes.

Signal Fly *Rivella species*

Often seen walking about on foliage, wings in constant motion (as if signaling). Look for the three wing bands that helps identify this family. A single larva develops inside a single root nodule of a legume. June to September.

Grass Flies (Frit Flies) Family Chloropidae

Appearance
Small, generally between ¹/₁₆ to ⅛ inch long, relatively hairless flies. Grass flies are often yellow and black or gray.

Biology
Grass flies are common in meadows and other grassy areas and are usually low on plants. They are often associated with living plants or decaying organic matter while some are predaceous and a few are a gall makers. Grass flies are common spring and summer.

Grass Fly *Chlorops species*

Tiny but colorful. Look for the grass flies in grasses and sedges near water. Yellow body with black markings. They not only lay eggs in grass stems but often feed inside the stems too. A swelling can appear. Encountered from May to August.

Stilt-legged Flies
Family Micropezidae

Appearance

Small to medium sized flies, measuring from ⅛ to ½ inch long. They have an elongate body and very long legs, especially the second and third pairs, and an abdomen narrowed anteriorly to a stalk. Stilt-legged flies can resemble wasps or ants. These flies are usually light brown or blue black.

Biology

Stilt-legged flies are usually found around moist sites in wooded areas, meadows, marshes, and similar areas, where they are typically found on leaves. These flies can have elaborate courtship rituals and lay eggs in rotting wood, fruit, or other decaying plant matter. In addition to their similarity to wasps, some stilt-legged flies mimic wasp behavior to further the appearance. Look for stilt-legged flies during May to August.

Stilt-legged Fly *Rainiera antennaepes*

When waving and rubbing their front legs out in front of their head, this stilt-legged fly mimics an ichneuman wasp with its twitching antennae. Often seen on vegetation. Striking with a blue black thorax and abdomen and brown legs. It is common June and July.

Black Scavenger Flies Family Sepsidae

Appearance

Small, $^1/_{16}$ to $^1/_4$ inch long, shiny black slender to medium-bodied flies. Black scavenger flies have a very round head, are ant-like or wasp-like and sometimes have a black spot on each wing near the tip.

Biology

Black scavenger flies are found in variety of habitats associated with decaying organic materials especially manure as well as carcasses and decaying plant matter. They have the curious habit of "rowing" their wings outwards as they walk. Black scavenger flies are common spring and summer.

Black Scavenger Fly *Sepsis species*

Antlike in appearance, the black scavenger flies have a black shiny black body and a dark spot at the tip of each wing. As they walk, they wave each wing independently of the other. Associated with dung and carcasses (hence their common name). Look for this group of black scavenger flies May into September.

Glossary

Abdomen: The elongated, eleven-segmented rearward body part.

Ametabolous Metamorphosis: A type of metamorphosis in which the adults are wingless and the only difference between nymphs and adults is size.

Arthropod: Animals that possess segmented bodies, a hard external integument (exoskeleton) and paired jointed appendages, e.g. legs and antennae (insects, spiders, ticks, mites, crayfish, centipedes and millipedes.).

Caudal Filaments: Long appendages at tip of abdomen, a.k.a "tails" (mayfly nymphs).

Cerci: A pair of appendages on the last segment of the abdomen that usually function as sensory organs.

Crepitation: rubbing peg-like structures on their back legs against their forewing producing a low buzzing song or by making a snapping sound with their wings as they fly.

Elytra: The first pair of wings modified into a hard shell (beetles).

Femur: Portion of the leg closest to the insect's body; above the tibia.

Furcula: A forked appendage used for jumping. When not in use, a furcula is tucked up under the body, set like a mouse trap. When released, it extends down rapidly propelling the insect forward (springtails).

Grub: Larval stage of some insects, especially beetles.

Hemelytrous Wings: Wings that are part leathery and part membranous (true bugs).

Hemimetabolous Metamorphosis: A type of metamorphosis in which the nymphs (sometimes called naiads) are aquatic and differ considerably in form from the adults which live on land.

Herbaceous Plants: Plants that have leaves and stems that die down to the ground at the end of the growing season; non-woody plants.

Holometabolous Metamorphosis: A type of complete metamorphosis in which larvae look very different from adults, usually feeding on different types of food and living in different habitats. Last instar larvae molt into a pupa or resting stage.

Honeydew: A sugary sticky waste material produced by aphids . Honeydew can be a food source of other insects, especially ants.

Hypermetamorphosis Metamorphosis: A rare type of metamorphosis in which the larva is alligator-like when is first hatches. This stage, called a triungulin, is very active. The following stages are grublike and inactive (blister beetles).

Instar: The stage between molts in an insect's life.

Maggot: The legless larvae of flies.

Mandibulate: Possessing mandibles.

Metamorphosis: A change in form during development. Sometimes this change is gradual but many times it is very dramatic.

Nymph: Immature stage of some insects (mayflies, dragonflies, etc.)

Ocelli: Simple eyes.

Ootheca: A case in which eggs are produced (cockroaches).

Ovipositor: Structure used by females to lay eggs in a suitable environment.

Palp: A segmented finger-like extension of the mouthparts.

Paurometabolous Metamorphosis: A type of metamorphosis in which the nymphs and adults are similar in form, differing chiefly in size, and typically live the same environment.

Proboscis: Extended, coiled mouthparts (butterflies, moths).

Prolegs: False legs on a larvae (caterpillars).

Pronotum: The dorsal (top) surface of the prothorax. Can be broad and plate-like in some insects (cockroaches, fireflies).

Prothorax: Front section of the thorax (e.g. the spined portion of a Spined Soldier Bug).

Reflex Bleeding: Secreting a noxious fluid from leg and body joints for protection from potential predators (ladybird beetles).

Puparium: Protective covering around the pupa (pl. puparia). The puparium often consists of the last shed larval "skin," darkened and hardened into a capsule-like envelope (flies).

Scutellum: A segment of the pronotum; often triangular (true bugs, beetles).

Stridulation: Sound produced by grasshoppers, crickets and katydids for mating, distress and aggression. Accomplished by rubbing specialized structures on two body parts together (orthopterans).

Thorax: Mid section of an insect consisting of the prothorax, mesothorax and metathorax. There is a pair of legs on each thoracic segment.

Tymbals: Sound organs located on the sides of the base of the cicada abdomen which vibrate and resonate into a cavity located inside parts of the thorax and abdomen (cicadas).

Tympanum: An ear in the tibia of the front legs (katydids).

Viviparous: Eggs develop inside the mother and she gives birth to live young (aphids).

Insect Websites

Insects of Cedar Creek google "cedar creek insects"
This central Minnesota Natural History Area has an extensive online collection of pinned specimens, phenology tables and much more information.

BugGuide www.bugguide.net
A great online resource for identifying your insect and spider photos.

Nearctic Database www.nearctica.com
Lists of all North American insects.

University of Minnesota Extension www.extension.umn.edu
Information on insects as it relates to home and gardening.

Photo Credits

Robert Dana: 117 d

Jeff Hahn: 17 b, 25 a, 28 a, 30 a, 31 b, 34 c, 35 ab, 36 ab, 37, 39, 41 ab, 43, 47, 50 c, 51 a, 52 ab, 54 acd, 56 a, 58 c, 59 b, 61 ab, 62 abc, 63 b, 64 c, 65 ab, 69 b, 71 ad, 73 ac, 74 a, 75 a, 76 b, 77 ab, 83 bd, 84 bd, 87 d, 88 bc, 90, 91, 92 b, 93 ab, 94 bc, 95, 96, 97 ab, 98 abc, 99 abc, 100 ab, 101 ac, 102 b, 103 a, 104 de, 105 b, 107 a, 110 ab, 111 c, 113 abc, 114 ab, 115 b, 116 b, 118 ab, 119 cd, 120 cd, 121 c, 122 bd, 123 acd, 125 b, 127 a, 128 bc, 130 d, 131 ab, 134, 135 ac, 137, 138 d, 143, 144 bc, 145 abc, 147 d, 148 abd, 149 ab, 151 a, 152 a, 155 ad, 157 a, 158 b, 160 a, 161 de, 162 c, 164 ab, 165 d, 169 ac, 171, 173 b, 174 a, 175 d, 177 ac, 178 bcd, 179 d inset, 180 a, 181 c, 184 ac, 185 bc, 189 bc, 190 ac, 191 ab, 194 ab, 198 bc, 199 b, 203 ac, 204 a, 205 bc, 207 c, 208 ac, 211 c, 213 ac, 215 c, 216 a, 217 bc, 220 c, 221 a, 222 b, 223 abc, 224 c, 226, 228 ab, 231 ab, 232

Dean Hanson: 25 b, 169 b

J. C. Lucier: 156 b

Tom Murray [www.pbase.com/tmurray74]: 23 a, 30 c, 32 acd, 33 ab, 48, 57, 66 b, 69 a, 71 c, 75 c, 109 a, 116 a, 135 bd, 138 a, 165 c, 168 abd, 230

Rod Planck: 58 a, 68 a, 82 a, 85 d, 131 c, 139 ab, 146 a, 206 b, 207 d, 213 d

Mike Reese [www.wisconsinbutterflies.org]: 31 c, 216 b

Allen Blake Sheldon: 89 b, 94 a, 109 d, 125 d, 126 a, 139 c, 146 b, 186 b, 190 b, 209 ab

Jim Sogaard: 142 c, 144 a, 182 ab, 183 abc, 184 b

Sparky Stensaas [www.sparkyphotos.com]: 10, 12 abc, 13 ab, 16 ab, 17a, 18 abc, 19 ab, 20 abcd, 21 abcd, 22 abc, 23 b, 25 c, 26, 28 b, 29 abc, 30 bd, 31 ab, 32 b, 34 b, 46, 49, 50 ab, 51 b, 53 ab, 54 b, 55 ab, 56 b, 58 b, 59 ac, 60 abc, 63 a, 64 ab, 65 cd, 66 ac, 67 ab, 68 bc, 70 ab, 71 b, 72 ab, 73 bd, 74 b, 75 bd, 76 a, 77 inset/c, 79 ab, 82 c, 83 ac, 84 ac, 85 abc, 86 abcd, 87 abc, 88 a, 89 a, 92 a, 93 c, 98 d, 99 d, 101 b, 102 a, 103 b, 104 abcf, 105 a, 106 ab, 107 b, 108 ab, 109 bc, 110 cde, 111 ab, 112, 115 a, 117 abc, 119 ab/inset, 120 ab, 121 abd, 122 ac, 123 b, 124 abc, 125 ac, 126 bcd, 127 bcd, 128 ad, 129 abc, 130 abc, 131 d, 135 e, 136 ab, 138 bc, 142 ab inset, 147 abc, 148 c inset, 150 abcde, 151 bc, 152 b, 153 abcd, 154 abcde, 155 bc, 156 a, 157 bcdef, 158 acd, 159 ab, 160 b, 161 abc, 162 ab, 163, 164 nest, 165 ab, 168 ce, 172 abc, 173 ac, 174 b, 175 abc inset, 176 ab inset, 177 bd, 178 a insets, 179 abc, 180 bc inset, 181 ab inset, 185 a, 186 a, 187 abc, 188 ab, 189 a, 192, 198 ad, 199 ac, 200 ab, 202 ab, 203 b, 205 a, 206 ac, 207 ab, 208 b, 210 abc, 211 abd, 212 abcd, 213 b inset, 214 ab, 215 abd, 217 ad, 218 ab, 219 abcd, 220 abd, 221 bc, 222 a, 224 ab, 225 ab, 227 abc, 228 c, 229 abc, 233 ab

Larry Weber: 34 a, 195, 199 d, 2018

Gene White: 118

Numbering begins at the top starting with "a" and proceeds down the page.

Titles of Interest

Acorn, J. and Sheldon, I. 2003. *Bugs of Ontario*. Lone Pine Publishing. Edmonton, AB. 160 pp.

Arnett, R. H., Jr. and Thomas, M. C. 2001. *American Beetles, Volume 1: Archostemata, Myxophaga, Adephaga, Polyphaga: Staphyliniformia*. CRC Press LCC, Boca Rotan, FL. 443 pp.

Arnett, R. H., Jr., Thomas, M. C., Skelley, P. E. and Frank, J.H. (editors). 2002. *American Beetles, Volume 2: Polyphaga: Scarabaeoidea through Curculionoidea*. CRC Press LCC, Boca Raton, FL. 861 pp.

Arnett, R. H., Jr. 2000. *American Insects: A Handbook of the Insects of America North of Mexico, 2nd Edition*. CRC Press LCC, Boca Raton, FL. 1003 pp.

Bland, R. G. 2003. *The Orthoptera of Michigan*. Michigan State University Extension Bulletin E-2815. East Lansing, MI. 220 pp.

Capinera, J. L., Scott, R. D. and Walker, T. J. 2004. *Field Guide to Grasshoppers, Katydid, & Crickets of the United States*. Cornell University Press, Ithaca, NY. 249 pp.

Covell, C. V., Jr. 2005. *A Field Guide to Moths of Eastern North America*. Virginia Museum of Natural History, Martinsville, VA. 496 pp.

Eaton, E. R. and Kaufman, K. 2007. *Kaufman Field Guide to Insects of North America*. Houghton-Mifflin. 391 pp.

Johnson, N. F. and Triplehorn, C. A. 2004. *Borrer and DeLong's Introduction to Insects, 7th Edition*. Thomas Brooks/Cole, Belmont, CA. 864 pp.

Marshall, S. A. 2006. *Insects—Their Natural History and Diversity: With a Photographic Guide To Insects of Eastern North America*. Firefly Books Ltd Buffalo, NY. 718 pp.

McAlpine, J. F., Peterson, B. V., Shewell, G. E., Teskey, H. J., Vockeroth, J. R. and Wood, D. M. 1981. *Manual of Nearctic Diptera, Vol. 1. Monograph No. 27*. Ottawa Research Branch, Agriculture Canada. 674 pp.; *Vol. 2, Monograph No. 28*. 1987. Ottawa Research Branch, Agriculture Canada. pp. 675 - 1332.

Mead, K. 2009. *Dragonflies of the North Woods*: 2nd Edition. Kollath-Stensaas Publishing. 193 pp.

Slater, J. A. and Alexander, J. 1978. *How To Know the True Bugs*. William C. Brown Company, Dubuque, IA. 256 pp.

Sogaard, J. 2009. *Moths and Caterpillars of the North Woods*. Kollath-Stensaas Publishing. 288 pp.

Weber, L. 2006. *Butterflies of the North Woods: 2nd Edition*. Kollath-Stensaas Publishing. 279 pp.

White, R. E. 1983. *A Field Guide to the Beetles of North America: Peterson Field Guide*. Houghton-Mifflin, Boston, MA. 368 pp.

Index

A

Acanalonia bivittata 69
acanaloniid planthoppers 69
Acanaloniidae 69
Acanthosomatidae 66
Acmaeodera pulchella 100
Acroneuria carolinensis 23
Acrosternum hilare 65
Actias luna 183
Adelphocoris lineaolatus 53
Admiral
—Red 178
—White 178
Aedes vexans 203
Aerial Yellowjacket 164
Aeshna canadensis 16
Aeshnidae 16
Agallia quadripunctata 74
Agapostemon splendens 151
Agonum cupripenne 84
Agonum placidum 84
Agrilus anxius 101
Agrilus planipennis 101
Agrilus ruficollis 101
Agriotes fucosus 102
*Agrothereutes abbreviator
    iridescens* 148
Alaus oculatus 103
Alder Leaf Beetle 119
alderflies 134
Alderfly 134
Alfalfa Plant Bug 53
Allocapnia species 25
Allograpta obliqua 220
Alydidae 62-63
Alydus eurinus 62
Alypia octomaculata 190
Ambush Bug, Jagged 59
ambush bugs 58-59
American Carrion Beetle 93
American Copper 175
American Emerald 18
American Sand Wasp 154
Ammophila species 157
Anasa tristis 61
Anatis mali 109
Anax junius 16
Anisosticta bitriangularis 110
Ant
—Carpenter 160
—False Honey 161
—Mound-building 161
—Pavement 161
—Velvet 159
Antheraea polyphemus 183
Anthocoridae 57
Anthomyiidae 223
Antlion 139
antlions 139
ants 160-161
Apateticus cynicus 64
Aphid

—Brown Ambrosia 77
—Greater Striped Red Oak 77
—Oleander 76
—Woolly Alder 77
Aphididae 76-77
aphids 76-77
Aphis nerii 76
Aphrophora parallela 73
Apidae 152-153
Apis melifera 152
Apple Maggot 229
Aquarius remigis 50
Arched Hooktip Moth 185
Archytas apicifer 227
Arctia caja 187
Arctic Skipper 180
Arctic, Jutta 179
Arctiidae 186-187
Arphia pseudonietana 31
Arphia sulphurea 32
Asilidae 210-213
Assassin Bug, Spined 59
assassin bugs 58-59
Athysansus argentarius 74
Atlantis Fritillary 176
Atylotus bicolor 207
Automeris io 182
Autumn Meadowhawk 21

B

Backroad Tiger Beetle 86
backswimmers 49
Bald-faced Hornet 164
Banasa dimidiata 64
Banasa Stink Bug 64
Banded Hairstreak 175
Bark Beetle, Red Flat 113
bark beetles 129-131
barklice 78-79
Barklouse 79
Baskettail, Common 18
Bean Leaf Beetle 120
Beautiful Tiger Beetle 85
bee flies 214-216
Bee Fly
—Greater 214
—Pygmy 214
—Sinuous 215
Bee Wolf 155
Bee
—Bumble 152-153
—Carpenter 153
—Digger 153
—Honey 152
—Leaf-cutting 150
—Small Carpenter 153
—Splendid Metallic Green 151
—Sweat 151
Beetle
—Blister 116-117

—Burying 93
—Carrion 92
—Checkered 107
—Click 102
—Clown 91
—Colorado Potato 121
—Darkling 115
—Dogbane 119
—Dung 96
—False Japanese 98
—Fire-colored 115
—Flat Bark 113
—Flea 121
—Forked Fungus 114
—Goldsmith 99
—Ground 83-84
—Japanese 98
—June 97
—Ladybird 108
—Larder 105
—Leaf 118-123
—Long-horned 124-128
—Milkweed 125
—Net-wing 103
—Oil 116
—Picnic 111
—Predaceous Diving 89
—Rove 94
—Sexton 93
—Soldier 106
—Spotted Cucumber 120
—Stag 95
—Sumac Flea 118
—Tiger 85-87
—Tortoise 123
—Tumbling Flower 113
—Water-lily 122
—Wedge-shaped 112
—Whirligig 88
—Woodland Ground 84
—Giant Water Scavenger 90
beetles 80-131
Belostomatidae 47
Bembidion confusum 83
Bembix americana spinole 154
Berytidae 60
Bibio species 204
Bibionidae 204
Big Poplar Sphinx 181
Bittacomorpha clavipes 200
Black & Yellow Lichen Moth 186
Black & Yellow Mud Dauber 157
Black Blister Beetle 117
Black Damsel Bug 56
Black Dancer 169
Black Firefly 104
Black Fly 202
Black Horse Fly 207
Black Onion Fly 230
Black Scavenger Fly 233
Black Swallowtail 172

Black-shouldered Spinyleg 17
Black-sided Grouse Locust 33
Blackhorned Tree Cricket 36
Blattaria 42-43
Blepharida rhois 118
Blister Beetle
—Black 117
—Gray 117
—Nuttall's 117
—Say's 117
blister beetles 116-117
blow flies 224
Blue Mud Dauber 156
Bluet, Familiar 22
Bog Copper 175
Boisea trivittata 63
Bolitotherus cornutus 114
Bombus fervidus 153
Bombus impatiens 152
Bombus ternarius 153
Bombyliidae 214-216
Bombylius major 214
Bombylius pygmaeus 214
booklice 78-79
Boreal Long-lipped
    Tiger Beetle 86
Boreidae 195
Borer, Bronze Birch 101
Borer, Divergent Metallic
    Wood 100
Borer
—Dogwood 191
—Elderberry 126
—Emerald Ash 101
—Locust 126
—Raspberry Cane 125
—Red-femured Milkweed 125
—Red-necked Cane 101
—Red-shouldered Pine 127
—Yellow-marked Metallic Wood 100
Boreus brumalis 195
Bottle Fly, Common Green 224
Boxelder Bug 63
Brachiacantha albifrons 110
Brachynemurus nebulosus 139
Broad-headed Bug 62
broad-headed bugs 62-63
Broadwinged Bush Katydid 34
Bronze Birch Borer 101
Bronzed Tiger Beetle 87
Brown Ambrosia Aphid 77
Brown Lacewing 137
Brown Mantidfly 136
Brown Water Scorpion 46
brush-footed butterflies 176-179
Buffalo Treehopper 71
Bumble Bee
—Common Eastern 152
—Golden Northern 153
—Orange-belted 153
bumble bees 152-153

Buprestidae 100-101
Burying Beetle 93
butterflies 172-180

C

Cabbage White 173
caddisflies 166-169
caddisfly larval cases 168
Caddisfly
—Long-horned 168
—Northern Casemaker 169
—Zebra 169
Calico Pennant 21
Caliroa cerasi 145
Calligrapha alni 119
Calligrapha multipunctata 119
Calligrapha rowena 119
Calliphoridae 224
Callosamia promethea 183
Calopteron terminale 103
Calopteryx aequabilis 22
Calosoma calidum 82
camel crickets 37
Camnula pellucida 30
Campaea perlata 184
Camponotus noveboracensis 160
Canada Darner 16
Canadian Tiger Swallowtail 172
Candy-striped Leafhopper 75
Cantharidae 106
Capsus ater 55
Carabidae 82-87
Carabus maeander 83
Carpenter Ant, New York 160
carpenter ants 160
Carrion Beetle
—American 93
—Margined 93
carrion beetles 92
Carterocephalus palaemon 180
Casebearing Leaf Beetle 121
Catocala amatrix 190
Cecropia Moth 183
Celastrina argiolus 174
Celithemis elisa 21
Cerambycidae 124-128
Cerastipsocus venosus 79
Ceratina species 153
Cercopidae 72-73
Cercyonis pegala 179
Ceresa alta 71
Ceresa basalis 70
Cerotoma trifurcata 120
Ceuthophilus maculatus 37
Chafer
—Rose 98
—Sand 98
Chalk-fronted Corporal 20
Chalybion californicum 156
Chauliodes rastricornis 135
Chauliognathus pennsylvanicus 106

Checkered Beetle, Red-Blue 107
checkered beetles 107
Checkerspot, Silvery 177
Chelymorpha cassidea 123
Chionea valga 199
Chironomidae 205
Chlaenius sericeus 84
Chloropidae 231
Chlorops species 231
Chlosyne nycteis 177
Chorthippus curtipennis 32
Chortophaga viridifasciata 30
Chrysanympha formosa 190
Chrysididae 159
Chrysochus auratus 119
Chrysomela scripta 120
Chrysomelidae 118-123
Chrysopa chi 138
Chrysopilus quadratus 208
Chrysopilus thoracicus 209
Chrysops species 206
Cicada Killer, Eastern 155
Cicada, Dogday 68
cicadas 68
Cicadellidae 74-75
Cicadidae 68
Cicindela
—*denikei* 85
—*duodecimguttata* 85
—*formosa* 85
—*lepida* 85
—*limbalis* 86
—*longilabris* 86
—*punctulata* 86
—*purpurea* 86
—*repanda repanda* 87
—*scutellaris lecontei* 87
—*sexguttata* 87
Cimbex americana 142
cimbicid sawflies 142
Cimbicidae 142
Citrus Planthopper 69
Clear-winged Grasshopper 30
clearwing moths 191
Cleridae 107
Click Beetle, Eyed 103
click beetles 102-103
Climaciella brunnea 136
Clostera albosigma 188
Clouded Sulphur 173
Clown Beetle 91
clown beetles 91
clubtails 17
Cluster Fly 224
Clytus ruricola 126
Coccinella septempunctata 108
Coccinella trifasciata 109
Coccinellidae 108-111
Cockroach, Wood 43
cockroaches 42-43
Coenus delius 65

Coleomegilla maculata 110
Coleoptera 80-131
Colias philodice 173
Collaria meilleurii 55
Collembola 10-11
Colorful Foliage Ground Beetle 83
Comma, Eastern 177
Common Baskettail 18
Common Damsel Bug 56
Common Eastern Bumble Bee 152
Common Green Bottle Fly 224
Common Green Darner 16
Common Oblique Syrphid 220
Common Pondhawk 21
common sawflies 144-145
common scorpionflies 194
Common Water Strider 50
Common Whitetail 20
Common Wood-Nymph 179
Condylostylus species 217
Conehead, Sword-bearing 35
Conocephalus fasciatus fasciatus 35
Convergent Ladybird Beetle 109
Copper
—American 175
—Bog 175
coppers 175
Coral Hairstreak 175
Coral-winged Grasshopper 32
Cordulia shurtleffii 18
Corduliidae 18
Coreidae 61
Corimelaena pulicaria 67
Corixidae 48
Corporal, Chalk-fronted 20
Corydalidae 134
Corydalus cornutus 135
Corythucha cydoniae 52
Cosmopepla lintneriana 65
Cosmosalia chrysocoma 128
Cotalpa lanigera 99
Cottonwood Leaf Beetle 120
Cow Path Tiger Beetle 86
Crabronidae 154-155
Crackling Locust 30
crane flies 198-199
Crane Fly
—Giant 199
—Giant Eastern 199
—Phantom 200
—Wingless 199
—Winter 201
Creophilus maxillosus 94
Crescent, Northern 177
Cricket
—Blackhorned Tree 36
—Fall Field 36
—Spotted Camel 37
crickets 36
Crocus Geometer 185
Ctenucha virginica 186
Cuckoo Wasp 159
Cucujidae 112-113
Cucujus clavipes 113
Cuerna striata 75

Culicidae 203
Curculio nasicus 131
Curculionidae 129-131
Cycloneda munda 110
Cylindromyia species 227

D

Damsel Bug
—Black 56
—Common 56
damsel bugs 56
damselflies 22
Danaus plexipus 179
Dancer, Black 169
Dark Fishfly 135
Dark-winged Fungus Gnat 205
Darkling Beetle, Roughened 115
darkling beetles 114
darners 16
Darner
—Canada 16
—Common Green 16
Dasymutilla species 159
deer flies 206-207
Deer Fly 206
Dermaptera 40-41
Dermestes lardarius 105
dermestid beetles 105
Dermestidae 105
Desmocerus palliatus 126
Diabrotica undecimpunctata 120
Diamond-backed Spittlebug 73
Diapheromera femorata 39
Dicerca divaricata 100
Dichelonyx subvittata 98
Digger Bee 153
Digger Wasp 155
Digger Wasp, Golden 158
digger wasps 154-155
Dineutus species 88
Diptera 196-233
Disonycha alternata 121
Disonycha pensylvanica 121
Divergent Metallic Wood Borer 100
dobsonflies 134-135
Dobsonfly 135
Dogbane Beetle 119
Dogday Cicada 68
Dogwood Borer 191
Dogwood Leaf Beetle 119
Dolerus apricus 144
Dolichopodidae 216-217
Dolichopus remipes 217
Dolichovespula arenia 164
Dolichovespula maculata 164
Donacia species 122
Dorocordulia libera 18
Dot-tailed Whiteface 21
dragonflies 14-21
Dragonhunter 17
Drepana arcuata 185
Drepanidae 185
Dromogomphus spinosus 17
Drone Fly 219
Dryocampa rubicunda 182

Dun Skipper 180
Dung Beetle 97
Dung Beetle, Earth-boring 96
dung flies 221
Dung Fly, Golden 221
Dusky Stink Bug 64
Dytiscidae 89
Dytiscus species 89

E

Earth-boring Dung Beetle 96
Earwig, European 41
earwigs 40-41
Eastern Cicada Killer 155
Eastern Comma 177
Eastern Forest Tent Caterpillar 189
Eastern Yellowjacket 165
Ectemnius species 155
Eight-spotted Forester 190
Elasmostethus cruciatus 66
Elasmucha lateralis 66
Elateridae 102-103
Elderberry Borer 126
Ellychnia corrusca 104
Elm Leaf Beetle 120
Elm Sawfly 142
Emerald Ash Borer 101
Emerald
—American 18
—Racket-tailed 18
emeralds 18
Enallagma civile 22
End Band Net-wing Beetle 103
Enoclerus nigripes nigripes 107
Enodia anthedon 179
Entylia carinata 71
Ephemeroptera 12-13
Epicauta fabricii 117
Epicauta pennsylvanica 117
Epiphragma fasciapenne 198
Epistrophe species 220
Episyron biguttatus 162
Epitheca cynosura 18
Erioptera chlorophylla 199
Eristalis dimidiata 219
Eristalis tenax 219
Erythemis simplicicollis 21
Erythroneura comes 75
Euaresta festiva 228
Eumenes fraternus 165
Euphyes vestris 180
European Earwig 41
Eurosta solidaginis 229
Eurygaster species 67
Euschistus tristigmus 64
Evodinus monticola 126
Exacaverus species 148
Exoprosopa fascipennis 215
Eye-spotted Ladybird Beetle 109
Eyed Click Beetle 103

F

Fall Field Cricket 36
False Honey Ant 161
False Japanese Beetle 98

Familiar Bluet 22
Feniseca tarquinius 174
Festive Fruit Fly 228
Festive Tiger Beetle 87
Fiery Hunter 82
Fire-colored Beetle 115
fireflies 104-105
Firefly
—Black 104
—Winter 104
fishflies 135
Fishfly
—Dark 135
—Spring 135
flat bark beetles 112-113
flatid planthoppers 69
Flatidae 69
Flea Beetle 121
flesh flies 225
flies 196-233
Flower Bug, Insidious 57
flower flies 218-221
Fly
—Bee 215-216
—Black 202
—Black Onion 230
—Black Scavenger 233
—Cluster 224
—Common Green Bottle 224
—Crane 198
—Deer 206
—Drone 219
—Dung 221
—Flower 218-221
—Friendly 225
—Fruit 228
—Goldenrod Gall 229
—Grass 231
—Horse 207
—House 222
—Hunch-backed 216
—Long-legged 217
—March 204
—Muscid 222
—Parasitic 226-227
—Phantom Crane 200
—Robber 210-213
—Root-maggot 223
—Signal 231
—Snipe 208
—Soldier 209
—Stable 223
—Stilt-legged 232
—Sunflower Maggot 229
—Winter Crane 201
Forester, Eight-spotted 190
Forficula auricularia 41
Forked Fungus Beetle 114
Formica species 161
Formicidae 160-161
Formosa Looper 190
Four-spotted Skimmer 19
Fourlined Plant Bug 54
Fourspotted Clover Leafhopper 74
Friendly Fly 225

frit flies 231
Fritillary
—Atlantis 176
—Great Spangled 176
froghoppers 72-73
fruit flies 228-229
Fruit Fly, Festive 228
Fungus Gnat, Dark-winged 205

G

Galerucella nymphaeae 122
gasteruptiid wasps 163
Gasteruptiidae 163
Gasteruption species 163
Geometer, Crocus 185
geometers 184-185
Geometridae 184-185
Geotrupes splendidus 96
Geotrupidae 96
Gerridae 50
Ghost Tiger Beetle 85
Giant Crane Fly 199
Giant Eastern Crane Fly 199
Giant Ichneumon 146
Giant Stonefly 25
Giant Water Bug 47
Giant Water Scavenger Beetle 90
Gladiator Meadow Katydid 35
Glischrochilus fasciatus 111
Gnophomyia tristissima 198
Golden Digger Wasp 158
Golden Dung Fly 221
Golden Northern Bumble Bee 153
Golden-backed Snipe Fly 209
Goldenrod Gall Fly 229
Goldenrod Leafminer 123
Goldenrod Soldier Beetle 106
Goldsmith Beetle 99
Gomphidae 17
Graceful Sedge Grasshopper 32
Grammia parthenice 187
Grape Leafhopper 75
Grape Pelidnota 99
Graphocephala coccinea 75
grass flies 231
Grass Fly 231
Grasshopper
—Clear-winged 30
—Coral-winged 32
—Graceful Sedge 32
—Green-striped 30
—Marsh Meadow 32
—Mottled Sand 31
—Northern Marbled 31
—Northwestern Red-winged 31
—Pygmy 33
—Sulphur-winged 32
grasshoppers 28-33
Gray Blister Beetle 117
Great Black Wasp 158
Great Spangled Fritillary 176
Great Tiger Moth 187
Greater Bee Fly 214
Greater Striped Red Oak Aphid 77

Green Immigrant Leaf Weevil 130
Green Lacewing 138
Green Stink Bug 65
Green-margined Tiger Beetle 86
Green-striped Grasshopper 30
Ground Beetle, Colorful Foliage 83
Ground Beetle, Minute 83
Ground Beetle, Pedunculate 83
Ground Beetle, Woodland 84
ground beetles 82-87
Grouse Locust, Black-sided 33
grouse locusts 33
Gryllus pennsylvanicus 36
Gyponana octolineata 75
Gyrinidae 88

H

Hagenius brevistylus 17
Hairstreak
—Banded 175
—Coral 175
hairstreaks 175
Hairy Flower Scarab 99
Hairy Rove Beetle 94
halictid bees 151
Halictidae 151
Haploa lecontei 187
Haploa, Leconte's 187
Harmonia axyridis 110
Harvester 174
Hawthorn Lace Bug 52
Helophilus species 219
Hemerobiidae 137
Hemerobius species 137
Hemipenthes sinuosa. 215
Hemiptera 44-77
Hesperidae 180
Heterosilpha ramosa 92
Hexagenia limbata 13
Hippodamia convergens 109
Hippodamia tredecimpunctata 109
Histeridae 91
Hobomok Skipper 180
Honey Bee 152
hooktip moths 185
Hornet, Bald-faced 164
hornets 164
Horntail, Pigeon 143
horse flies 206-207
Horse Fly, Black 207
Hoshihananomia octopunctata 113
House Fly 222
Hunch-backed Fly 216
Hyalophora cecropia 183
Hybomitra lasiophthalma 207
Hydrophilidae 90
Hydrophilus triangularis 90
Hydrophorus species 217
Hylemya alcathoe 223
Hyles lineata 181
Hylobius warreni 131
Hymenoptera 140-165
Hypogastrura nivicola 11

IJK

Ichneumon clasma 147
ichneumon wasps 146-149
Ichneumon, Giant 146
Ichneumonidae 146-149
Insidious Flower Bug 57
Io Moth 182
Isodontia mexicana 156
Issidae 69
Jagged Ambush Bug 59
Jalysus wickhami 60
Japanese Beetle 98
Jewelwing, River 22
Judolia montivagans 127
June Beetle 97
Jutta Arctic 179
Katydid
—Broadwinged Bush 34
—Gladiator Meadow 35
—Slender Meadow 35
katydids 34-35

L

Labidomera clivicollis 118
Lace Bug, Hawthorn 52
Lacewing
—Brown 137
—Green 138
lacewings 137-138
Ladona julia 20
Lady, Painted 178
Ladybird Beetle
—Convergent 109
—Eye-spotted 109
—Multicolored Asian 110
—Seven-spotted 108
—Spotless 110
—Spotted 110
—Thirteen-spotted 109
—Three-banded 109
—Two-triangled 110
ladybird beetles 108-111
ladybugs 108-111
Lampyridae 104-105
Laphria
—*canis* complex 212
—*cinerea* 212
—*flavicollis* 212
—*huron* 212
—*janus* 213
—*posticata* 213
—*sacrator* 213
—*sericea / aktis* complex 213
Lappet Moth 189
Larder Beetle 105
Large Lace-border Moth 185
Large Whirligig Beetle 88
Lasiocampidae 189
Lasioglossum species 151
Laurentian Tiger Beetle 85
Leaf Beetle
—Alder 119
—Bean 120
—Casebearing 121

—Cottonwood 120
—Dogwood 119
—Elm 120
—Long-horned 122
—Many-spotted 119
—Striped Willow 121
—Swamp Milkweed 118
—Tenspotted 122
—Water-lily 122
leaf beetles 118-123
leaf-cutting bees 150
leaf-footed bugs 61
Leafhopper
—Candy-striped 75
—Eight-lined 75
—Fourspotted Clover 74
—Grape 75
—Silver 74
—Striped 75
leafhoppers 74-75
Leafminer, Goldenrod 123
Lebia species 83
Leconte's Haploa 187
Lepidophora lepidocera 216
Lepidophora lutea 216
Lepidoptera 170-191
Leptoceridae 168
Leptoglossus occidentalis 61
Leptura plebeja 127
Leptura subhamata 127
Lepyronia quadrangularis 73
Lepyrus palustris 129
Lestes rectangularis 22
Lethocerus americanus 47
Leucorrhinia intacta 21
Libellula
—*luctuosa* 20
—*pulchella* 19
—*quadrimaculata* 19
Libellulidae 19-21
Lichen Moth, Black & Yellow 186
lightning bugs 104-105
Limenitis arthemis arthemis 178
Listronotus delumbis 130
Lixus caudifer 129
Locust Borer 126
Locust, Crackling 30
long-horned beetles 124-128
Long-horned Caddisfly 168
Long-horned Leaf Beetle 122
long-legged flies 216-217
Looper, Formosa 190
Lucanidae 95
Lucanus placidus 95
Lucidota atra 104
Lucilia sericata 224
Luna Moth 183
Lycaena epixanthe 175
Lycaena phlaenas americana 175
Lycaenidae 174-175
Lychomorpha pholus 186
Lycidae 103

Lygaeidae 60
Lygaeus kalmii 60
Lygus lineolaris 54
Lytta nuttalli 117
Lytta sayi 117

MNO

Machimus notatus 211
Macrodactylus subspinosus 98
Macrosiagon dimidiata 112
Macrostemum zebratum 169
Maggot, Apple 229
Malacosoma disstria 189
mantidflies 136
Mantidfly, Brown 136
Mantisipidae 136
Many-spotted Leaf Beetle 119
march flies 204
March Fly 204
Margined Carrion Beetle 93
Marsh Meadow Grasshopper 32
Mayflies 12-13
Meadow Plant Bug 53
Meadow Spittlebug 73
Meadowhawk
—Autumn 21
—White-faced 20
Mealworm, Yellow 114
Mecoptera 192-195
Megachile species 150
Megachilidae 150
Megacyllene robiniae 126
Megalotoma quinquespinosus 62
Megarhyssa atrata 146
Megarhyssa macrurus 146
Melanotus species 102
Melissodes species 153
Meloe species 116
Meloidae 116-117
Membracidae 70-71
Mesembrina species 222
metallic wood-boring beetles 100-101
Metcalfa pruinosa 69
Metriorrhynchomiris dislocatus 54
Microgoes oculatus 125
Micropezidae 232
Microrhopala vittata 123
midges 205
Milbert's Robber Fly 210
Milbert's Tortoiseshell 177
Milkweed Beetle, Red 125
Milkweed Bug, Small 60
Milkweed Tortoise Beetle 123
Minute Ground Beetle 83
minute pirate bugs 57
Miridae 53-55
Monarch 179
Monochamus notatus 124
Monochamus scutellatus 124
Mononychus vulpeculus 130
Mordellidae 113
mosquitoes 203

Moth
—Arched Hooktip 185
—Black & Yellow Lichen 186
—Cecropia 183
—Io 182
—Lappet 189
—Large Lace-border 185
—Luna 183
—Polyphemus 183
—Promethea 183
—Rosy Maple 182
moths 181-191
Mottled Sand Grasshopper 31
Mound-building Ant 161
Mourning Cloak 178
Mud Dauber
—Black & Yellow 157
—Blue 156
Multicolored Asian Ladybird
    Beetle 110
Musca domestica 222
muscid flies 222-223
Muscidae 222-223
Mutillidae 159
Myrmeleontidae 139
Mystacides sepulchralis 169
Myzocallis bellus 77
Nabicula subcoleoptrata 56
Nabidae 56
Nabis americoferus 56
Necrophila americana 93
Negro Bug 67
Nematus species 144
Nemognatha lutea lutea 116
Nemotaulius hostilis 169
Neoconocephalus ensiger 35
Neoitamus orphne 211
Neomyia cornicina 223
Nepidae 46
Net-wing Beetle, End Band 103
Neuroptera 132-139
New York Carpenter Ant 160
Nicrophorus species 93
Nigronia fasciata 135
Nigronia serricornis 135
Nitidulidae 111
Noctuidae 190
Northeastern Sawyer 124
Northern Casemaker Caddisfly 169
Northern Crescent 177
Northern Marbled Grasshopper 31
Northern Paper Wasp 165
Northern Pearly-eye 179
Northern Walkingstick 39
Northwestern Red-winged
    Grasshopper 31
Notodontidae 188
Notonecta species 49
Notonectidae 49
Nut Weevil 131
Nuttall's Blister Beetle 117
Nymphalidae 176-179
Nymphalis antiopa 178

Nymphalis milberti 177
Oberea bimaculata 125
Odonata 14-22
Odontomyia cincta 209
Oecanthus nigricornus 36
Oenis jutta 179
Oiceoptoma noveboracense 93
Oil Beetle 116
Okanagana rimosa 68
Oleander Aphid 76
Oligocentria semirufescens 188
Olive-winged Drake 13
One-eyed Sphinx 181
Onthophagus hecate 97
Ophion nigrovarius 148
Ophraella conferta 123
Orange-belted Bumble Bee 153
Orchelium gladiator 35
Orius insidiosus 57
Orthoptera 26-37
owlet moths 190

PQR

Pachybrachis species 121
Pachysphinx modesta 181
Painted Lady 178
Pale Beauty 184
Panorpa species 194
Panorpidae 194
Paper Wasp, Northern 165
paper wasps 165
Papilio canadensis 172
Papilio polyxene 172
Papilionidae 172
Paracharactus rudis 145
Paraprociphilus tessellatus 77
parasitic flies 226-227
Parcoblatta species 43
Pardalophora apiculata 32
Parent Bug 66
Parhelophilus rex 218
Paroxyna albiceps 228
Parthenice Tiger Moth 187
Pavement Ant 161
Pear Sawfly 145
Pearly-eye, Northern 179
Pedicia albivitta 199
Pedilus species 115
Pedunculate Ground Beetle 83
Pelecinid Wasp 149
Pelecinidae 149
Pelecinus polyturator 149
Peleteria species 227
Pelidnota punctata 99
Pelidnota, Grape 99
Pennant, Calico 21
Pentacora ligata 51
Pentatomidae 64-65
Phaenicia sericata 224
Phantom Crane Fly 200
Phasmida 38-39
Philaenus spumarius 73
Philanthus ventilabris 155

Photuris pennsylvanica 105
Phyciodes selenis 177
Phyllodesma americana 189
Phyllophaga species 97
Phymata pennsylvanica 59
Physonota helianthi 123
Picnic Beetle 111
picture-winged flies 230
Pieridae 173
Pieris rapae 173
Pigeon Horntail 143
Pigeon Tremex 143
Pine Spittlebug 73
Plant Bug
—Alfalfa 53
—Fourlined 54
—Meadow 53
—Tarnished 54
plant bugs 53-55
Planthopper
—Citrus 69
—Two-striped 69
Plateumaris species 122
Plathemis (Libellula) lydia 20
Platydracus cinnamopterus 94
Platystomatidae 230-231
Plecoptera 23-25
Plume Moth 191
Poanes hobomok 180
Podabrus species 106
Podisus maculiventris 65
Poecilanthrax alcyon 215
Poecilocapsus lineatus 54
Poecilognathus sulphureus 216
Poecilus chalcites 84
Polistes fuscatus 165
Pollenia rudis 224
Polydrusus sericeus 130
Polygonia comma 177
Polyphemus Moth 183
Pompilidae 162
Pondhawk, Common 21
Popillia japonica 98
Potter Wasp 165
Predaceous Diving Beetle 89
Prenolepis imparis 161
Proctacanthus milbertii 211
Proctacanthus rufus 210
Promethea Moth 183
Prominent
—Red-washed 188
—Sigmoid 188
prominents 188
Protenor belfragei 63
Psocus leidyi 79
Pteronarcys species 25
Pterophoridae 191
Ptilodexia species 226
Ptychopteridae 200
Pycnocryptus director 149
Pygmy Bee Fly 214
Pygmy Grasshopper 33
pygmy grasshoppers 33

Pyrochroidae 115
Racket-tailed Emerald 18
Rainiera antennaepes 232
Ranatra fusca 46
Raspberry Cane Borer 125
Red Admiral 178
Red Flat Bark Beetle 113
Red Milkweed Beetle 125
Red-Blue Checkered Beetle 107
Red-crossed Stink Bug 66
Red-femured Milkweed Borer 125
Red-necked Cane Borer 101
Red-shouldered Pine Borer 127
Red-washed Prominent 188
Reduviidae 58-59
Rhagio mystaceous 208
Rhagionidae 208-209
Rhagoletis pomonella 229
Rhopalidae 63
Rhyssa species 147
Ripiphoridae 112
Rivellia species 231
River Jewelwing 22
robber flies 210-213
Robber Fly
—Milbert's 211
—Three-banded 211
Root-maggot Fly 223
Rose Chafer 98
Rosy Maple Moth 182
Roughened Darkling Beetle 115
Rove Beetle, Hairy 94
rove beetles 94

S

Salda species 51
Saldidae 51
Saldula species 51
Sand Chafer 98
Sand Wasp, American 154
sapfeeding beetles 111
Saprinus species 91
Sarcophaga aldrichi 225
Sarcophagidae 225
Saturniidae 182-183
Satyrum calanus 175
Satyrum titus 175
sawflies 142-145
Sawfly
—Elm 142
—Pear 145
Sawyer
—Northeastern 124
—White-spotted 124
Say's Blister Beetle 117
scarab beetles 97-99
Scarab, Hairy Flower 99
Scarabaeidae 97-99
Scarites quadriceps 83
Scathophaga stercoraria 221
Scathophagidae 221
Sceliphron caementarium 157
scentless plant bugs 63
Sciaridae 204-205

Scopula limboundata 185
scorpionflies 192-195
Scorpionfly 194
Scorpionfly, Snow 195
Scudderia pistillata 34
Scutelleridae 67
Searcher 83
Seed Bug, Western Conifer 61
seed bugs 60
Sepsidae 233
Sepsis species 233
Sericomyia militaris 219
Sesiidae 191
Seven-spotted Ladybird Beetle 108
Sexton Beetle 93
Sharp-lined Yellow 184
shield bugs 67
shore bugs 51
Sialidae 134
Sialis velata 134
Sicya macularia 184
Sigara species 48
Sigmoid Prominent 188
signal flies 230-231
Signal Fly 231
Silphidae 92
Silver Leafhopper 74
Silvery Checkerspot 177
Simulidae 202
Simulium species 202
Sinea diadema 59
Sinuous Bee Fly 215
Siricidae 143
Six-spotted Tiger Beetle 87
Skimmer
—Four-spotted 19
—Twelve-spotted 19
—Widow 20
skimmers 19-21
Skipper
—Arctic 180
—Dun 180
—Hobomok 180
skippers 180
Slender Meadow Katydid 35
Slender Spreadwing 22
Small Carpenter Bee 153
Small Milkweed Bug 60
Small Winter Stonefly 25
Smerinthus cerisyi 181
Smicronyx constrictus 131
snipe flies 208-209
Snipe Fly, Golden-backed 209
Snow Flea 11
Snow Scorpionfly 195
Snowfly 25
Soldier Beetle, Goldenrod 106
soldier beetles 106
Soldier Bug, Spined 65
soldier flies 209
Soldier Fly 209
Speyeria atlantis 176
Speyeria cybele 176
Sphaerophoria species 221

Spharagemon collare 31
Spharagemon marmorata marmorata 31
Sphecidae 156-158
Sphecius speciosus 155
Sphex ichneumoneus 158
Sphex pensylvanicus 158
Sphingidae 181
sphinx moths 181
Sphinx
—Big Poplar 181
—One-eyed 181
—White-lined 181
spider wasps 162
Spilomyia fusca 218
Spined Assassin Bug 59
Spined Soldier Bug 65
Spined Stilt Bug 60
Spinyleg Willowfly 25
Spinyleg, Black-shouldered 17
Spittlebug
—Diamond-backed 73
—Meadow 73
—Pine 73
spittlebugs 72-73
Splendid Metallic Green Bee 151
Spotless Ladybird Beetle 110
Spotted Camel Cricket 37
Spotted Cucumber Beetle 120
Spotted Ladybird Beetle 110
Spreadwing, Slender 22
Spring Azure 174
Spring Fishfly 135
Springtails 10-11
Squash Bug 61
Stable Fly 223
Stag Beetle 95
Staphylinidae 94
Stenotus binotatus 53
Stethophyma gracile 32
Stichopogon trifasciatus 211
Stictoleptura canadensis 127
Stilt Bug, Spined 60
Stilt-legged Fly 232
Stink Bug
—Banasa 64
—Dusky 64
—Green 65
—Red-crossed 66
—Two-spotted 65
stink bugs 64-65
Stomoxys calcitrans 223
stoneflies 23-25
Stonefly
—Giant 25
—Small Winter 25
Strangalepta abbreviata 128
Strangalia acuminata 128
Stratiomyidae 209
Strauzia species 229
Strigoderma arbicola 98
Striped Leafhopper 75
Striped Willow Leaf Beetle 121
Sulphur-winged Grasshopper 32

Sulphur, Clouded 173
sulphurs 173
Sumac Flea Beetle 118
Sunflower Maggot Fly 229
Sunflower Tortoise Beetle 123
Swallowtail
—Black 172
—Canadian Tiger 172
swallowtails 172
Swamp Milkweed Leaf Beetle 118
Sweat Bee 151
Sweetheart Underwing 190
Sword-bearing Conehead 35
Sympetrum obtrusum 20
Sympetrum vicinum 21
Synanthedon scitula 191
Syrphid, Common Oblique 220
Syrphidae 218-221
Syrphus species 220

T

Tabanidae 206-207
Tabanus atratus 207
Tabanus species 207
Tachinidae 226-227
Taeniopteryx species 25
Tarnished Plant Bug 54
Telamona molaris 71
Telamona monticola 71
Tenebrio molitor 114
Tenebrionidae 114
Tenspotted Leaf Beetle 122
Tent Caterpillar, Eastern Forest 189
tent caterpillars 189
Tenthredinidae 144-145
Tenthredo species 145
Tephritidae 228-229
Tetramorium caespitum 161
Tetraopes femoratus 125
Tetraopes tetrophthalmus 125
Tetrigidae 33
Tetrix arenosa 33
Tettigidea lateralis 33
Theronia species 148
Thirteen-spotted Ladybird
     Beetle 109
thread-waisted wasps 156-158
Three-banded Ladybird Beetle 109
Three-banded Robber Fly 211
Three-lined Potato Beetle 121
Thyreocoridae 67
Thyreodon atricolor 147
Tibicen canicularis 68
Tiger Beetle
—Backroad 86
—Beautiful 85
—Boreal Long-lipped 86
—Bronzed 87
—Cow Path 86
—Festive 87
—Ghost 85
—Green-margined 86
—Laurentian 85
—Six-spotted 87

—Twelve-spotted 85
tiger beetles 85-87
Tiger Moth
—Great 187
—Parthenice 187
tiger moths 186-187
Tiger Swallowtail, Canadian 172
Tingidae 52
Tipula abdominalis 199
Tipulidae 198-199
Tortoise Beetle
—Milkweed 123
—Sunflower 123
Tortoiseshell, Milbert's 177
Toxomerus geminatus 220
Toxomerus marginatus 220
Treehopper, Buffalo 71
treehoppers 70-71
Tremex columba 143
Trichiotinus assimilis 99
Trichiotinus piger 99
Trichocera species 201
Trichoceridae 201
Trichodes nutalli 107
Trichodosia albovittata 184
Trichoptera 166-169
*Trimerotropis verruculata
     verruculata* 30
Tritoxa flexa 230
true flies 196-233
Tumbling Flower Beetle 113
Twelve-spotted Skimmer 19
Twelve-spotted Tiger Beetle 85
Two-spotted Stink Bug 65
Two-striped Planthopper 69
Two-triangled Ladybird Beetle 110
Tychius species 131
Typocerus velutinus velutinus 128

UVW

Ulidiidae 230
Underwing, Sweetheart 190
Upis ceramboides 115
Uroleucon ambrosiae 77
Vanessa atalanta 178
Vanessa cardui 178
Velvet Ant 159
Vespidae 164-165
Vespula maculifrons 165
Villa lateralis 215
Virginia Ctenucha 186
Walkingstick, Northern 39
walkingsticks 38
Warren Root Collar Weevil 131
Wasp
—American Sand 154
—Cuckoo 159
—Digger 155
—Gasteruptiid 163
—Golden Digger 158
—Great Black 158
—Pelecinid 149
—Potter 165
—Spider 162

—Thread-waisted 156
Water Boatman 48
Water Bug, Giant 47
Water Scavenger Beetle, Giant 90
Water Scorpion, Brown 46
Water Strider, Common 50
Water-lily Beetle 122
Water-lily Leaf Beetle 122
Wedge-shaped Beetle 112
Weevil
—Green Immigrant Leaf 130
—Nut 131
—Warren Root Collar 131
weevils 129-131
Western Conifer Seed Bug 61
Whirligig Beetle, Large 88
White Admiral 178
White-faced Meadowhawk 20
White-lined Sphinx 181
White-spotted Sawyer 124
White-striped Black 184
White, Cabbage 173
Whiteface, Dot-tailed 21
whites 173
Whitetail, Common 20
Widow Skimmer 20
Willowfly, Spinyleg 25
Wingless Crane Fly 199
Winter Crane Fly 201
Winter Firefly 104
Wood Cockroach 43
Wood-Nymph, Common 179
Woodland Ground Beetle 84
Woolly Alder Aphid 77

XYZ

Xanthogaleruca luteola 120
Xanthonia decemnotata 122
Xanthotype species 185
Yellow Mealworm 114
Yellow-marked Metallic Wood
     Borer 100
Yellow, Sharp-lined 184
Yellowjacket
—Aerial 164
—Eastern 165
yellowjackets 164-165
Zebra Caddisfly 169
Zelus exsanguis 59
Zygoptera 22

Quick Insect Finder

Ambush & Assassin Bugs	58	Ladybird Beetles	108
Ants	160	Leaf Beetles	118
Aphids	76	Leafhoppers	74
Bee Flies	214	Long-horned Beetles	124
Blister Beetles	116	Mayflies	13
Bumble Bees	152	Moths	181
Cicadas	68	Paper Wasp	164
Cockroaches	43	Plant Bugs	53
Crane Flies	198	Robber Flies	210
Crickets	36	Snow Fleas (Springtails)	11
Damselflies	22	Stink Bugs	64
Dragonflies	16	Stoneflies	25
Fireflies	104	Swallowtails	172
Grasshoppers	28	Sphinx Moths	181
Honey Bee	152	Tiger Beetles	85
Hornets	164	Treehoppers	70
Ichneumons	146	Walkingstick	39
Katydids	34	Wasps	164

Other user-friendly field guides from Kollath+Stensaas Publishing

Lichens of the North Woods
Joe Walewski

Dragonflies of the North Woods
Kurt Mead

Orchids of the North Woods
Kim & Cindy Risen

Moths & Caterpillars of the North Woods
Jim Sogaard

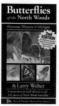

Butterflies of the North Woods
Larry Weber

Spiders of the North Woods
Larry Weber

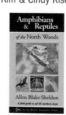

Amphibians & Reptiles of the North Woods
Allen Blake Sheldon